#Are Here

How To STFU and Show Up For Yourself

Dr. Tony Ortega

First published by Ortus Press,
an imprint of Free Association Books.

A CIP Catalogue of this book is available from
the British Library

ISBN: 978-1-91138-332-1

Typeset by
Typo•glyphix
www.typoglyphix.co.uk

Cover design by
Carroll Associates

Printed and bound in England

Acknowledgements

To Helen Lewis: You wear so many titles in my life, but the one that means the most is Guardian Angel. Thank you for always believing in me even when I didn't.

To Harry Crosland and the folks at PopCultureUncovered.com: Thank you for giving this crazy geek a platform to express himself in his unique way, which gave birth to the path I've been on. I am forever grateful.

To Alisia Leavitt: You continue to be the OBGYN/ surrogate mother/midwife of my creative endeavors. I'm glad we are so crazy together.

To Jennifer Safrey: Thank you for not only being one of my biggest cheerleaders but by always keeping me looking so good.

To Mark Dominic: Girl, I can't make this without your crazy eidetic memory of yours. Always can count on you to identify the source of the most obscure quotes.

Thanks for always having my back even when I don't want you to.

To that publisher (who will remain nameless) that turned this book down because I didn't have a strong enough online platform: Thank you for reminding me never to give up, even when my social media following is subpar. As Cher said in "Burlesque," You haven't seen the last of me.

To all the personal development programs and self-help gurus I've spent so much money on over the years: Thanks for the inspiration to write a book on not needing y'all.

To all my peeps, too many to point out singly: Thank you for sticking by me during a very trying time post-publication of #IsHeHereYet. You are my backbone.

To that Power greater than myself, whom I choose to call God: Your sense of humor never ceases to amaze me. I have a blessed life, so thank you.

Dedication

In Loving Memory Of
Ron Winter

You were one of the best and in a short time, you
left one hell of an impact. We miss you Dorothy. Thank
you for being a friend. I love you.

"That through the radiance which was once so bright
be now forever taken from my sight. Though nothing
can bring back the hour of splendor in the grass, glory
in the flower. We will grieve not, rather find strength in
what remain behind."

William Wordsworth

Foreword

Have you ever been attracted to the exciting flurry
of a new self-help movement, only to find yourself
disappointed and crashed out a few months later? Ever
found yourself spending a lot of money on a program
that promises to help you to be your Best You, only to
leave you feeling like the same you that you started
with? If you are like millions of people, including Dr.
Tony Ortega, then you have ridden the roller coaster
of spiritual highs and lows many times only to find
yourself constantly discouraged, drained, and even
nauseous afterward.

Fortunately, Dr. Ortega is declaring an end to this
cycle, and sharing his simple, effective, and no-
nonsense approach to true self-wellness and healing. By
withdrawing power and attention away from the gurus,
and returning true empowerment and loving energy
toward the individual, Dr. Ortega is drawing a spiritual
line in the sand against inauthentic leaders and vacuous
self-help movements. He outlines ways the reader can
find their own voice, create their own truth, and live
their very best life out loud.

STFU demonstrates how YOU can be the guru, the healer, the hero, the saviour of your own life. It lovingly but firmly places YOU as the expert of your own healing and wellness. It disregards the smoke and mirrors of the profitable self-help industry and instead shows you how to authentically shine (and save a lot of money!). By doing so, Dr. Ortega creates real possibilities for change, growth, pleasure, and peace.

Damon L. Jacobs,
Licensed Marriage and Family Therapist,
author of "Absolutely Should-less" and "Rational Relating."

Introduction

The quest for personal improvement is almost as pervasive as the one for love. We have become a society obsessed on improving ourselves, yet never seem to get there. Just like with any obsession, this requires an outside source to feed it.

If you think about the current state of the self-improvement world (or even the world in general), we are continually bombarded with advertisement of products, either in the form of online coaching, online courses, multi-level marketing ventures, in-person seminars, etc. The fitness industry has seen revenue like never before. The level at which we have become inundated with self-improvement has conditioned us to think we need to improve ourselves all the fucking time. We have become so inundated with ways to better ourselves that it has caused an undercurrent of shame if you do not participate. It's almost like a brainwashing. The message is: "If you don't do this, you won't look/feel/do better."

Once the self-help community was all about helping one another. Now it's become a business with lots of competitors.

Follow me here: We have an underlying desire to improve ourselves. We are flooded with ways and means to do so. All of them cost money. Let's do it. Let's improve ourselves. Oh, we can make money off it if as well. You mean I can be my best self and make some coin? Give me some, Mary.

This is happening because we *want* to improve ourselves. We *want* to be better. We *want* to be like everyone else. Yet, what do we get when we achieve THAT level of self-improvement? We get told we have still more work to do through this course/book/teacher/product. It is a never-ending quest.

When is enough going to be enough? As with any obsession, it's never enough.

Some of the undercurrents that fuel our quest include not feeling good enough and wanting to be a part of something. I felt like this as a kid and still do to this day, at times. When I embarked on the most serious mission to improve myself (despite already

2

having a doctorate degree in psychology, living in New York City, and working for a prestigious psychology firm), I dove into the deep end. Despite having all the knowledge I had acquired over the years and the very obvious career successes, I still felt like I didn't belong and that there was at least *something* off with me. I also didn't feel like I belonged as I was a bit of a loner and, as you can imagine, I am not your traditional mental health professional.

I got on my horse and started my quest. There was so much out there and I wanted it all. I read every book. I attended more seminars than a drag queen has makeup. I was so hungry and thirsty. New York City and the online community were my candy store and I was going full-blown diabetic coma.

I completed a curriculum that promised me the world. What I ended up getting was a deep dislike of this particular organization and all the people involved. As long as the check cleared and you signed up for their next course before you finished the one you were doing, it was all good. If you did not, you were wrong and you clearly did not care for the next level of your transformation. Thankfully I have the character defect—or asset—of being very stubborn and saying no when pushed into a corner. They were trying to sell me transformation but when I would not drink the Kool-Aid, I was shamed for not continuing to spend the time and money on their products.

I read so many books and met so many of the authors. I hit it off really well with one of them and ended up going to all of their live seminars. This person also had a very strong following and I made so many friends. This internationally known speaker valued me (or so they said). I thought I had found my tribe and my mentor. I volunteered at every one of this person's events. They even promised me that they would help me with some projects that would propel my career into a different direction while introducing me to important folks. When I needed this person, they weren't there, as they had promised they'd be even when I hadn't ever asked. I got the excuse, "too busy doing …" But I saw that they weren't like that with others. What was wrong with me? And there I went again, thinking there was something wrong with me. Why wasn't I part of their "It" crew?

When I spoke up about this (granted, I can sometimes be quite uncouth), their followers—including some of my alleged friends—went for my jugular. It seemed like I was no longer part of the tribe as I had dared say something negative against this person. My true friends stuck around (and are still here). Otherwise, I was no longer the valued member of the family I once was. I was left with the feeling of not being good enough and not belonging. My quest ended me in the same spot I was in prior to starting. I had read the books, done the course, and bought the products, and I felt the exact same way as I had when I started.

No, I think I felt worse.

I'd done the fucking work. I'd read all the books. I'd attended all the seminars. I'd *done* the fucking work. Why didn't I get the results I wanted? It was supposed to work. I did all the right things. Why did my life suck so badly?

And that's when I said, "Tony, STFU and show up for yourself. Remember all that big talk about being the person you want to be with? Here's your chance."

It is, and always will be, about being the one and focusing on the work I need to do to achieve my goals.

People started to come forward discreetly with similar stories of this person, as well as other so-called leaders. They shared emails and text/direct messages from folks who were treating their students like absolute shit. You mean, other people were doing the work and still feeling like they hadn't done shit? It was scary how cultish and corporate the personal development community had become. The conditioning we have been covertly given has taken hold on a global level. The consumers were all falling for this bullshit. Promises made were rarely kept. I wasn't alone in noticing the state of the self-improvement world. It was time to finally STFU and show up for ourselves.

In my greatest moments, I have come up with amazing solutions to work through whatever problem I was encountering. I didn't have to run to a famous person or something external to me. I had to go *in*. Sure, my support would offer guidance and help, but at the end of the day, they were not the end-all be-all of my "salvation." And while there are products and services I could use to augment my personal work, I had to make that decision on my own. Not be shamed or coerced into doing so. I had to show up for myself as I always had. I forgot who I was in my quest for self-improvement. No product, program, or celebrity has to tell me otherwise. No subtle shaming or aggressive sales tactics. It all boiled down to me. This is how I showed up for myself. Remembering who I am.

I fell prey to all the promises of a better life because I thought I didn't have one already. I loved the idea of being taught to attract everything I wanted by thinking good thoughts, when I already had that ability. It felt so good to belong to a tribe when I could have always been part of a tribe or started one of my own. Yeah, I forgot to show up for my own self.

What I came to realize in all of this was that I had it all wrong. Everything I needed, I already had. I just needed to STFU and show up for myself. When I did that, my compulsive reliance on external things becomes a thing of the past and I emerge powerfully (and less whiny). You would think that with a doctorate degree in psychology and 27 years of experience in the mental health field, I would know better. Still, though I had the knowledge, the covert programming of the self-improvement industry sabotaged my ability to personally apply this knowledge. Studies and statistics are great. However, without personal application of these results, they end up just being numbers.

What you hold in your hands is your guide to personal application of shutting the fuck up and showing up for yourself, Tony Ortega style. Think critically. Allow yourself to sit with new information before acting on it. The best thing to do to show up for you is not take yourself and everything else so seriously. Therefore, I hope to provide you with a few laughs along this journey.

You will notice that each chapter will include some #OMG Moments. These are the highlights of that section and the most important points to remember. Use these as your mantras. Make pretty affirmation cards. Now you don't have to worry about having a highlighter or pen on you to refer to key points in the chapter. I did it for you. You're welcome.

You will also find Utility Belt techniques. I named these after Batman's utility belt. He has no superpowers but sometimes he needs to have something within his reach to help him with the battle. Time to put on that cowl and say, "I'm Batman."

At the end of every chapter, have a seat and a refreshment with Tea Time with Tony. Who doesn't like some tea served piping hot? This is where the personal application of shit really hits home. Here, you will go from knowing something intellectually to KNOWING something within your whole being. You get to look at yourself when no one is around and get real with yourself. These questions will prompt you to show up for yourself in a way you probably never have. Don't worry about the results. No one is really going to know the answers unless you tell them.

Some questions to conclude with:

★ Are you tired of doing all the latest self-improvement stuff and getting little results or results that don't last very long?

★ Have you tried to be this huge MLM person and not reached the levels of success others have?

★ Are you just over being in the hamster wheel of this book, this product, and this teacher?

Well, Are You Here Yet? No? Then STFU and show up for yourself.

CHAPTER ONE
The Work of Being You... and Deciding to Work it Fierce

"It's your outlook on life that counts. If you take yourself lightly and don't take yourself too seriously, pretty soon you can find the humor in our everyday lives.

And sometimes it can be a lifesaver."

Betty White

Ah, today is so great. I just finished reading (insert self-help book title) and I know what to do to grab life by the balls and just feel good all the time. God, this is such an amazing feeling. I just want to hug everyone and skip instead of walk. But can I keep this up? OMG, did you see that? That fucking jerk just cut me off. The hell with *this self-help mumbo-jumbo. People are just shit and the world is cruel. I'm outta here.*

We have done the work, read great books, practised the principles, and made a commitment to be this amazingly positive person all the time. Then, that ONE person, that *ONE* event happens, and we are knocked off kilter. We go into a spiral of self-absorbed rage towards a relentlessly cruel world. And we ask ourselves, "Is it really worth it?"

STFU. You know it is.

Today's world is very focused on outcome-driven goals. Usually this outcome is of a material nature. Study hard to get the degree and that high-paying job so I can brag about it over brunch with my single miserable friends. Save up money for that house-share in Fire Island over the summer so I can bang as many dudes as I can. Diet and exercise to fit into that dress for so-and-so's wedding, which my ex will be attending. Get that new BMW so I can drive down the strip looking cool. Etc., etc. We do all this work and when we don't get the results, we want to throw in the towel.

Or here are some other scenarios:

You've attended this life-changing seminar and

within one week of completing it, you feel miserable again for no reason.

You finally finished that famous author's game-changing book that everyone is reading, yet you find you are not getting the results that the author (and everyone else) is talking about.

You have been meditating and doing yoga every day, but your boss is still an arsehole.

Or how about when it's just day-to-day shit? Not being able to find a seat on a crowded subway and this tourist gives you side eye because your backpack is too bulky. Your cable company is a piece of crap and you missed the season finale of *Modern Family*.

Don't get me wrong. I have been there many times.

> **#OMG Moment:** The point is that, no matter what the material outcome, it isn't ever why we need to be doing something in the present moment.

Sure, it's nice, but it can't always be the only goal. What we do needs to reflect who we really want to be, not what society wants us to be.

So much has been written about mindfulness and staying in the present moment. Here's what I will tell you in simple terms: THE PRESENT IS EVERYTHING. The past is over and cannot be undone. However, in the present, we can change our perceptions of the past and heal it. The future is yet to happen. However, in the present, our actions, choices, and behaviours will have a direct impact on how the future unfolds. So not only is staying in the present important for the sheer fact that it is really the only moment that exists; it also reshapes our past and shapes our future.

The other issue that contributes to our inability to stay in the moment is the infernal question, "What if?" *What if I do all this work and nothing happens?* Folks, if we focus hard enough, we will come up with 100 "what if" scenarios. Shit, I can do at least seventy-five in about three minutes. The question isn't "What if?" The question is "What now?" I love that question when I am working with clients. I assume clients come in to change aspects of their lives that aren't working. And I get it—change can be quite scary. Doing things differently and living in the present as mindfully as possible is a task that is tantamount to me having sex with a woman again.

Think about it, though. How we do things doesn't always work. We seek assistance to find different ways of doing things, and when we receive said assistance, we want to argue its validity.

I remember an old Alcoholics Anonymous (AA) saying (and they have the best sayings): "Nothing changes if nothing changes." Nothing will work if we don't try. If we try and it doesn't work, then we try something different. The point is to allow the ever-evolving nature of our being to exist. One very significant way to do this is to stop trying to control what everything is going to look like 24/7.

Our mental, emotional, and spiritual selves are like physical muscles. Just as our physical bodies need the repetition of certain movements to master them, so do our other bodies. This calls for a level of vigilance to the present moment that we are just not used to. We are so preoccupied with the end goal all the time, we essentially become greyhounds going after that rabbit. Time to stop chasing that rabbit and invite it in for a beer.

I see how we get so stuck in the past. I see it with my clients and, truth be told, in myself. I remember a motivational speaker saying one time, "The problem with traditional psychotherapy is that it allows people to whine, 'If my mother hadn't done this … if my father hadn't said that …'" She ended her tale by saying, "Well, you got it now."

So how do you work it fierce despite the everyday bullshit that makes you crazy?

★ **The paradox is giving a shit and not giving a shit.** If you give less shits to how something is supposed to look and give more shits to how you want to feel and show up in the world, you get to work it. It reminds me of a gym crush I had many moons ago. I would watch him work out and wonder, "He's not all that cute. Why am I so into him?" The answer was that he was walking around giving a shit and not giving a shit. He wasn't there for any pretence or accolades. He was there for his fitness and he just owned it. It was so palpable. (I know you have seen folks like this and wonder why you are so drawn to them.)

★ **When you engage in a new way of being or doing, don't judge yourself when you fuck it up.** Just start over. Another lovely AA saying I remember is, "Just for today." Folks in Twelve-Step programmes have easy ways to stay in the moment. Their philosophy is not to worry about staying sober for the rest of their lives but staying sober just for today. If just for today is too much to handle, then break it down even further to a block of hours. And if even that is too much, then stay sober for just one hour. You get my drift? If your day has been super overwhelming and what you really want to do is to cut a bitch, then stop and stay present for the next sixty minutes or just tell yourself that the day is starting over right now.

★ **Don't be afraid to acknowledge that you're pissed off.** Own it as much as you can, but don't stay in it. The difference is in shrugging your shoulders and saying to yourself, "Yeah, this really fucking sucks." Don't judge that feeling because you don't want to bypass your feelings with self-empowerment mumbo-jumbo. Own it. Now, that's fierce. However, follow that up by considering what could work for next time (and next time may be within the next hour or the next day). You can also acknowledge that it would be nicer if it looked like another way. It's okay to daydream and get in the feeling of what you would rather have instead of this. Today is not forever. This moment will pass.

Just acknowledge how it is and make an active choice to work it fierce.

★ **Go more by how you want to live.** I personally love to eat healthy and be a moderately fit fifty-year-old dude. However, come Sunday brunch, I love me some French fries and Bloody Mary cocktails. I stay in my "how". Now, if it means it keeps me in shape and I score hot dudes, well, that's the cherry on the ice cream sundae. If we live according to what *we* value and not necessarily what society values, we will work it fierce. Now, I am not advocating for a totally hedonistic way of life—just one in which you know how you want to show up in the world.

As you're reading this, you may be like, "Yeah, yeah, this all sounds great. How will this look in real life?" You asked for it and here is your first Utility Belt tool:

Step 1: Stop the bullshit talk.

Step 2: Check yourself.

Step 3: Choose differently.

Step 4: Walk the runway like you own it.

> **#OMG Moment:** When things go wrong, don't let bullshit talk start to occur. It keeps you in place of being basic, which is no good ... because, honey, you are better than basic.

People tend to have this all-or-nothing thinking where everything is all good or all bad. Things just *are*. Personal judgement of good and bad is just that: personal. Once the negative chatter comes to a dull murmur, it's time to check yourself. This means getting real with how things objectively are in the moment, not how you think they are at the moment. Get out of your own way and evaluate the situation for what it is *out there.*

> **#OMG Moment:** Choice is the one thing we ALWAYS control.

No matter what happens, we always have the power of choice. At any given moment, you can choose differently and/or choose again. We can get all woo-woo and say, "I choose love instead of fear," or we can just say, "I choose to not let this get to me so powerfully." It boils down to one thing: what you choose. After having completed the first three steps, walk down that runway like you just won *RuPaul's Drag Race*. Does this need any clarification, folks? What is fiercer than walking down a runway and owning that shit?

When you apply consistent practice of this concept and these steps, you will begin to realise one thing: you have the knowledge and the skills already to live fiercely in the face of any adversity. We have been able to apply these skills and knowledge in other areas. The key is to make it more generalisable. The pity party we engage in can give us attention and validation, but it also builds upon our already malignant victim mentality. STFU and show up for yourself.

Recently, I had a week in which I was just not living the way I wanted to, and I wanted things to look a certain way. I wasn't working it fierce per se, but was allowing things to unfold. Then I had several wins in the area of validation. Guys were paying more attention to me. My agent was creating me a bunch of opportunities for me to gain more exposure. I was doing well with my fitness regimen. Superficial for some but I will take the win. Sometimes a win isn't all that bad. It definitely can recalibrate us back to our value-driven path—but be careful to not let it be the driving force.

CASE STUDY

*Jackson – The Man Who Couldn't Go Out
Because What Would The Neighbours Think?*

Jackson was a lovely young man who came to see me initially because he was having trouble coming out as a gay man. He was so preoccupied with how others would perceive him that he was denying his essential self. He clearly was not working it fierce. With time, he was able to come out to his family and his closest friends. I was even able to work with him to go to a coming-out group and he started to develop friends who were gay men. However, there was still work to be done.

Jackson's groups and therapy sessions were always weekday evenings. Come the weekend, he wouldn't leave the house. He was always projecting that if his neighbours found out he was gay, they would all be talking about him. Jackson felt it would just be safer if he stayed in and not have to explain to anyone why he was coming home at 2 a.m. on a Saturday.

He began learning how to work it fierce and stay in the present moment. All his fears were future-based thoughts that would likely never come to pass (unless you live above my downstairs neighbour, because that bitch is Gladys Kravitz). I had him envision how he wanted to show up for his own life as he had the tools to do so. We worked on getting him laser-focused on how he wanted to live in the moment. Did that look like going to a gay bar with his friends on a Saturday?

Sometimes the notion was too overwhelming, so I had him just focus on the time it took to leave his home and get to the subway. I would then work with him to increase the time allotment and, eventually, Jackson was an active social person on the weekends. Did the neighbours have anything to say? We don't know, and Jackson started to not care as much. This is how he wanted to live, and he was working it.

Tea Time with Tony

1. *What are you doing for yourself on a daily basis to keep you on track with your stated goals and ways of being? If nothing, we have some work to do.*

2. *What are some things you wish you didn't have (i.e., experiences, etc.)? How can you see these as springboards for personal growth instead of complaining about them all the time?*

3. *How does asking, "What if?" benefit you? (And it does because we wouldn't keep asking it if we didn't benefit from it somehow.)*

4. *What knocks you out of the present moment the most? Is it not getting what you want? Results not looking the way you would want them to?*

5. *What material outcomes are you striving to achieve? What emotional needs are you thinking they will meet and how can you meet them differently?*

6. *What are some ways that you can stay in the present that you have tossed away in the past but can try again differently today?*

7. *What are the ways of being that really drive you? In other words, if, given all the tools and abilities (which you likely already have), how would you show up in the world?*

So, there you have it. Yes, life can suck and suck hard. However, this does not mean you need to be knocked out of the present moment and throw in the towel because it does suck. Do the daily work to at least keep you vigilant to what your path is, no matter who or what pisses you off. Then focus on more value-driven behaviour instead of material outcomes. This means identifying how you want to show up in the world. You can make the active choice to acknowledge your pain and resistance but also make the choice to say yes to life and to the present moment.

Get it now? Well, let's talk about something else that may piss you the fuck off: relationships. Follow me to Chapter Two where we explore: "So, your relationships suck ... It's Not the End of the World."

CHAPTER TWO
So, Your Relationships Suck ... It's Not the End of the World

"So, pick me, choose me, love me."

Dr. Meredith Grey, *"Grey's Anatomy"*

Somewhere in my travels I heard, "Relationships suck and then you die." Certainly not the most life-affirming of things to hear but, hey, haven't we felt that way at least once in our lives? For so many years of my life, I was not desperately seeking Susan, but a relationship. I even had myself so convinced I was doomed to be single that I inevitably created that reality. No, not because I am a mystic wizard, but because that thought led to certain behaviours which would drive away potential suitors. (BTW, that's how the Law of Attraction and manifesting *really* work. It's not magic; it's cognitive and behavioural.)

So along came the life experiences that led to the creation of my first book and once that was done and out in the market, I was like, "Hey, now, come and get me, boys." The boys did not show up as I had planned, and the dates that did show up were so emotionally unavailable that I was just over it quickly. I would even question whether I wanted a relationship or not. I thought I had arrived, so why was everything still the same?

Who are my folks out there who think they have done so much work to get a relationship, but it hasn't taken off? I am raising my hand with you, folks. Here is your challenge then: why did you do the work?

> **#OMG Moment:** When we don't see results in an area of our lives, we need to take a step back and either look at what we need to do differently and/or the motives behind why we did the work in the first place.

Let's talk about motives first. If, hypothetically speaking, my motive for losing weight is to have more sex, then when I start having more sex, I stop doing the work because I am getting what I wanted. The consequence of that is I may eventually stop getting the result I worked so hard for. Also, if our motives are not "pure" at their core, the work we are doing is quite half-arsed. I am not referring to virginal or religious purity; I'm talking about motives that are in alignment with who I want to be and how I want to show up in the world, not just a great bod and trick pelvis. Our behaviours towards the goal will be more in line with that goal if our motives are as we say they are.

We can sometimes believe we are doing something for one reason, but we are only fooling ourselves. That's not to say we can't have secondary motives. However, I know I have to get very clear about what I want a relationship to represent in my life.

I'll be an example. For me, relationships were always a hole filler (literally and figuratively). Relationships meant I was like everyone else. I was tired of folks asking about a plus-one when I didn't have one and it seemed everyone else did. Every time a holiday rolled around, I wanted to avoid most events, as I did not have a partner while most others at the festivities did. Therefore, I would approach relationships from a space of incompleteness. This led to behaviours consistent with me being incomplete, as how can I walk around and behave like someone who doesn't need a relationship to complete them when I do? For you *Grey's Anatomy* fans, I was the proverbial Meredith Grey. "Pick me, choose me, love me."

When I approach relationships from the perspective of complementing my life, I walk around whole and complete; therefore, my behaviour is consistent with a whole being, not with a being that needs to fill a hole (I'm loving this whole/hole thing, aren't you?). The bad news is that even if you are walking around with a sense of wholeness (see what I did there?), it does not guarantee results.

> **#OMG Moment:** Being true to your motives and walking around as a complete being only guarantees progress towards the goal, not necessarily the goal itself.

In a recent session with a client, I found myself saying, "It's not the goal that is the result, but the work is the result itself." Every time we make strides and take action towards the desired outcome, it creates psychological musculature that makes the chances of the desired outcome much greater. How do you keep your motives pure in regard to relationships? Here is the number one thing to always remember in *any* relationship that will prevent your own personal apocalypse.

#OMG Moment: Relationships are meant to complement your life, not complete your life.

Some of you may be saying, "So Meredith Grey had it wrong all this time?" Yes, my friends, she did. If you approach relationships from the perspective of completing you, no matter how hard you try, very subtle actions and words will manifest, and the other person will catch on to it. This is applicable for job interviews, social functions, and/or first dates. (For more on this, check out Chapter 9 of my book, *#IsHeHereYet*.)

Let's say you are one of those folks who think relationships complete you. You arrange a first date with someone. How do you carry yourself physically? Do you

overdo it on your makeup/perfume/dress to make sure
you impress? Do you analyse and pick apart what it is
that you are going to say on this date? At the end of the
date, are you obsessing over when the second date will
be? When you are home after the date, do you pick apart
everything you said and did, everything they said and
did? Yeah, you are using relationships to complete you.

In my first book, I made the analogy that first
dates need to be treated like job interviews to ease
the tension. That did not go over very well on Twitter
(which is fine by me, as I dislike Twitter and rabid
Twitter users immensely). However, I am able to take
feedback and check myself (more on that in the next
two chapters). Okay, I get it, maybe a job interview
wasn't the most appropriate analogy. What you are
looking for in a first date is someone that complements
your current complete life (again, this goes for a job
and/or other social situations).

Listen, in my fifty-one years of life and my twenty-
six years career as a mental health professional, I get it.
We do the work and we expect outcomes. We do the
work and we think we have arrived. Or we do the work
and think nothing has taken off. Why are we marking
major life events by the romantic or non-romantic
relationships we may or may not have?

> **#OMG Moment:** You do the work to be the work, not the results.

If you do the work, at some point you will get the results. The whole notion of looking up at a proverbial God and saying, "Okay, I've done the work, when is it coming?" was the inspiration for the title of my first book. When we do the work with the proper motives and in alignment with who we want to be, the results will come. We just never know when. Sorry, not sorry. And once you do get the results, the skills you built in the process of getting the result will be the foundation for all the maintenance work you will need to do to keep said result.

Much like physical personal training, if you work out with good form and maintain good eating, your muscles will grow, guaranteed. Even when you get to the desired muscle size, there is a level of maintenance that needs to happen, at the very least to stay at the level you are at. So, do we ever reach a stage where we have made it? Sure, but then the IT changes, no?

> **#OMG Moment:** Whether you have the outcome or not, or whether or not you are wanting to keep the outcome, you still have some level of work to do, so why not just do it?

This chapter's Utility Belt Strategy will work whether you are in a relationship or not.

Step 1: Query.

Step 2: Identify.

Step 3: Implement.

If you are single, your query is, "What do I need to do differently?" If you are not single, your query is, "What do I need to do differently?" If you are single, your identifying questions are, "How do I do this? How does it look like in the outside world?" If you are in a relationship, your identifying questions are, "How do I do this? How does it look like in the outside world?" If you are single and you have done your query and identifying steps, put it into action. If you are in a relationship and you have done your query and identify steps, put it into action.

Wait, did Tony just repeat the same thing for single and coupled folks? I sure did. Reason being the only difference between single and coupled individuals is the relationship status. The same work needs to get done; however, how it looks like in the real world may be quite different depending on relationship status.

The bottom line is: whether we are in a relationship or not, the one status that needs to change is our mental status, not the status on Facebook. Everything we do in life requires, at minimum, a shift in the way we perceive the circumstance. How many coupled folks do you know who are in miserable relationships? How many single people do you know who are thriving? The difference between these two sets of individuals is not their relationship status but their mental perspective. One chooses to stay in a bad situation for the sake of being in a relationship and the other chooses to use their current state to make themselves a better person.

A little tidbit to make relationships suck less: add more friendships into your romance and more romance into your friendships. No, I am not suggesting you have sex with your friends, silly. I am saying that by adding more romance to your friendships, we elevate them to a level at which they are as important as romantic relationships, taking the pressure off our partners (or the need to have one to live life more fully and completely). Conversely, by adding more friendship into our relationships, we then have more fun with the whole concept of intimacy and it makes it so much less scary. I say this as aren't we usually more scared of a romantic breakup than a friend breakup?

At the end of the day, whether romantic or otherwise, every relationship is an assignment. We learn from everyone we meet and every experience we have. It comes with the human condition. We have no choice in this unless we choose not to learn. We also get to choose whether we want to choose from a space of love or pain. We would be better off if we chose to learn through love, starting with ourselves first. The bad news and the good news are always the same; the only things we ultimately control are the choices we make. With everything else, we have to be content to do the work and surrender the outcomes to a power greater than us.

CASE STUDY
Sandy – The Girl With Fifty First Dates

Sandy came to my office to work on relationship issues. Boy, did she find the right place! Sandy had the ability to attract a lot of first dates but very little ability to follow up with second dates. Sandy was an attractive woman who was thriving in her profession. However, as she was getting into her thirties, societal pressures and biological factors were creating a sense of urgency to get into a relationship. Since she had difficulties getting a second date most of the time, the time was ripe for Sandy to do a deep dive into her relationships and how she had been going about them.

At times, I thought I was talking to the female version of me. When Sandy spoke about relationships, you would think the woman felt totally incomplete without one. However, based on her family and cultural background, it was no surprise she had this notion of relationships ingrained into her DNA. But before undoing some of these familial scripts, I thought it would be more prudent to take a tour of her head before, during, and after a date.

So, Sandy meets suitor. Great. She is giddy with excitement. She feels like a high school girl getting asked to her prom by the football captain. She keeps looking at the pics she was sent and wonder how good they would look together. She starts obsessing about her outfit for her first date. Sandy then starts to question if this is the right match for her. She has yet to go on the date.

On the date, her heart starts to beat fast. She is mega concerned her suitor won't like her, so she has to do more to guarantee he will. She stumbles on words and uses phrases indicating she is really wanting this to go in a relationship direction, and not in a subtle way. At the end of the date, she makes sure she gets an affirmation of a second date. That night, she stays up all night to analyse the date. Along with this, she picks out china patterns, wedding first-dance songs, potential neighbourhoods with good schools for kids, and possibly a divorce attorney. I am only exaggerating a tad, in case you are wondering.

Sandy had to rewrite first and foremost that relationships are not the end all, be all of her existence. She had to first do the work to *be* the person she wanted to be *with*. This would lay the foundation for the right and perfect partner to come in and be able to stay without feeling the pressure from her sense of incompletion. Sandy also required a lot of coaching to continue doing the work despite not having immediate outcomes, and to embrace the idea that the work is always worth it.

Last I heard from Sandy, she was able to get that partner of her dreams, keep the relationship stable and sane, and was in the process of artificial insemination to have a child with her partner. She did and continued doing the work.

Tea Time with Tony

1. *What do relationships mean to you? Do they complete you or complement you?*

2. *When you engage in any kind of personal development work, do you stay true to your motives or do you fall off the wagon for motives that will provide instant gratification?*

3. *What has made you give up on personal development work in the past?*

4. *Do you jump the gun on first dates? Take a look at when you transformed from runway model to basic bitch.*

Do relationships still suck for you? Good. Relationships do suck but they can also mean so many other things. It can mean you get to be present with your true intentions and live in that space. You get to learn so many great ways of being and doing. You gain freedom to be you in a loving space. You add on so many positive things you would have otherwise not had. Lastly, relationships always make the work worth it.

Now, on to tackle some ways in which we do ourselves a lot of damage and how to prevent it in Chapter Three, "Social Media: Check Yourself … Before You Wreck Yourself."

CHAPTER THREE
Social Media: Check Yourself ... Before You Wreck Yourself

"Am I the first one to get this cut? Because I'm working on becoming an Instagram influencer and I refuse to show my full asscrack, so my hairstyle needs to be on point."

Coco St. Pierre Vanderbilt,
"American Horror Story: Apocalypse"

Facebook. Twitter. Instagram. Tumblr. Snapchat. Stop the insanity, people. Don't we have enough? Social media these days makes me long for the simple days of MySpace. As I sit here writing this, I've likely just checked to see if my fave Instagram male celebrity just posted shirtless pic number 782 because the first 781 weren't enough.

We stay connected with family and friends on social media. We get the majority of our news on social media. We stalk our exes on social media (for the record, I've never, ever done this). Exes stalk us on social media (for the record, this has happened to me, mainly with my last ex). We do live educational feeds to make the world a better place. We take pictures of every fucking thing we eat, wear, travel to, experience, and so on for the whole world to see. My mother posts videos of Chihuahuas all day long on Facebook (love you, Mom).

Aren't we better people as a result of social media? Sadly, social media has turned us, for the most part, into a bunch of basic bitches.

In a later chapter, I'll discuss how social media almost ended my writing career. For the purposes of this chapter, I want to talk about one of the biggest dangers that social media stimulates: COMPARISON. Comparison occurs when we think we haven't met our goals or we are just coasting or we are not doing enough, or any combination of the three. Since we have become a society that emotionally vomits everything on social media, we know everything about everyone. The question that needs to be asked, though, is: are we getting an accurate representation?

One prime example is a fairly popular social media coach who claims to be a multi-millionaire. This person always posts pictures of themselves in exotic places they travel to, as well as with all the expensive designer stuff they buy. They are quite popular, yet had a pretty severe substance-related arrest behind the scenes that their followers knew nothing about for a while. They claim they outed themselves to be honest, but I think it's because they got tired of the posts of their mugshots being made public on—you guessed it—social media. So here you go: a social media celebrity advertising this amazing life, but clearly there is something not so great going on behind the scenes that led to an arrest. Things that make you go hmm ...

What's funny is when I first met this person, I really liked them. We had similar backgrounds and thought we could be friends and I could learn from them. I thought maybe I was doing something wrong because I was not travelling to exotic places nor buying designer stuff. I started to compare myself to them and think there was something I could be doing differently. As I kept comparing myself to them, I felt shittier about myself. The measuring stick was out, and it was not measuring me in my favour. Then it dawned on me: I make enough money that I can travel to exotic places and buy designer stuff. I choose not to because it's not who I am. I am not a travel-to-Mykonos-and-wear-Louis-Vuitton kind of gay. I am more the H&M and New York Comic Con kind of gay and I am super happy with that.

> **#OMG Moment:** The danger of social media is the subtle and covert way it tells you what you are doing and who you are being is wrong.

As time went on, I kept getting this nagging feeling that it was all a big scam, that this person was fake AF. Everything was revealed with this arrest and while I hope they are doing better since the arrest (we've not spoken in quite a bit), I want nothing of what they have because what I have is real for me. I am not better than them and vice versa. It just took me a bit to remember it.

This is just one of many examples of how social media has fucked with my head or, at least, what people post has. How much of your day is consumed with checking social media? Don't you think you will obtain a certain level of subconscious programming from what you see? It's like watching too much porn. You start to think sex actually looks like that, when a twenty-minute scene you view actually took hours and many takes to make. With enough exposure to anything, you make new connections in your brain to think in alignment with that exposure.

How many of you can recite the chorus for "I Will Survive" or do the "YMCA" dance moves? Have you ever had one of those mornings when you got to work and really didn't remember your commute? These things happen (and all of you who said yes to "I Will Survive" and "YMCA" are amazing human beings) because we do them so often they become literally second nature. One of my biggest struggles when I quit smoking cigarettes was what to do with my hands. When we do something often enough, physically and/or mentally we become it—and this includes our social media consumption.

#OMG Moment: Don't judge your insides by someone's outsides. Especially if it's the outsides they post on social media.

Think critically when consuming your social media. Shit, think critically about this book, too. If all your friends' posts are about themselves and how fabulous their lives are, chances are it's bullshit. Nobody has such a fabulous life 24/7.

Here is how you can think critically during your consumption of social media: look at their posts. Are they carefully staged, e.g., is there a designer handbag in *every* pic they post? Are their pics always in exotic locales? Is everything written always super positive and/ or fishing for compliments? Does it feel like they are trying to sell you something by showing off what they have? Are they asking you to like, follow, and repost? Lastly, does the drivel they write sound trendy? You guessed it: you found a social media celebrity and not a real person.

Most companies seeking to hire prominent social media celebrities (I use the word prominent as an adjective as these so-called celebrities have over 10,000 followers and are really nobodies) don't care about the quality of a person or the product, but about the "online platform" the individual has. Social media following has become more important than quality folks. Why? It's a numbers game. You post stuff, real or fake, that will garner the most responses and your following grows.

Companies save a ton of money in marketing and advertising by using "social media celebrities" to market their product. Conversely, if the "social media celebrity" has a product to sell, a major company will not pick it up unless the "celebrity" has a huge following. "Likes" run the world, sadly.

#OMG Moment: It's always quantity over quality on social media.

Are there real people on social media anymore? Fortunately, there are, and here are a few pointers to identify them: if you see posts about how they are overcoming stuff, even if it's stupid shit, read the content of their suggestions or experiences. If it sounds real, it may be real. Maybe they posted a picture of themselves first thing in the morning before morning coffee and brushing their hair. They rarely have a product in hand or speak about a service/programme they are taking. They don't ask questions like, "Do these Speedos make me look fat?" when they are clearly walking off the set of a Calvin Klein shoot. Real people on social media just share and share from the heart.

The biggest danger in comparing yourself to others via their social media is that you are comparing the movie of your life against their movie trailer. Film companies will only put the best scenes in a movie trailer. The same goes for most individuals on social media. While you do have some folks who could probably benefit from therapy and having their phone cut off, folks do tend to just put what they want you to see on social media. It is quite the superficial and fickle beast.

> **#OMG Moment:** Social media is not an accurate representation of someone's life, as it can be staged for profit and other purposes.

Now you know how to spot the fakes from the reals. However, you find yourself scrolling and scrolling mindlessly when you could be doing something else. What can you be doing differently? Limit your social media consumption to specific chunks of the day or specific time frames. My job is great because I can only scroll through social media between client sessions, which is usually just about ten minutes out of every hour, but I have to respond to calls and emails so there's that obstacle. Tell yourself you will only scroll during your lunch break or at home before dinner (which may cause indigestion). You may want to say, *I will only look at social media for a total of an hour a day* and log in your time every time you scroll.

> **#OMG Moment:** Don't consume social media first thing in the morning and/or right before bed.

Our minds are so much more susceptible to shit first thing in the morning. Try this experiment: wake up first thing in the morning and turn on the news or access news channels online and read/listen while you put on a pot of coffee. Start responding to those pesky emails. See what your friends posted on social media. Get to work fighting rush-hour traffic. Tell me you are not borderline homicidal by noon. You have essentially programmed your mind, when it is the most absorbent, with as much negativity as the modern world can provide. Your day is essentially shot to hell. You come home and you try to unwind. Whether you are single or married, you will have to deal with some sort of household stressors. You take your phone or tablet to bed and unwind by scrolling through social media. How did you end up sleeping that night?

If you learn anything from this chapter, please use some of the tips on when to use and when not to use social media. Do not be so robotic about your social media consumption. By being more mindful of your time online, you may be able to better combat the comparison that occurs.

I believe we have lost sight of what social media was initially intended for. (Except my mom. She's always posted dog videos on Facebook.) Check yourself before you wreck yourself by tuning in to why you are using social media. If you are old enough to remember MySpace, it was just a fun platform to post pictures and animated GIFs and so on. I don't recall any drama ensuing on there (unless you count my idiot cousin who always bitched that she was not in my Top Ten friends list). It just seemed like it was a nice place to share, not compete and compare. Post videos of Chihuahuas all day long and your life will be so much better (like my mom's).

Create an active intention for your use of social media. Be clear on what you are using it for. While not always sticking to this formula, these are my intentions: Facebook is purely personal. I share stuff on all my interests and make my sarcastic inquiries to folks who follow the page. Instagram is my jam because I don't want to read too much. I just want to look at pretty pictures (pretty pictures of shirtless men, but that's a whole other story). It's connected to a business Facebook page, so all my IG posts automatically go to that business page. Instagram is also the platform I use most for business stuff. Twitter I find mostly useless, but I participate just by posting but rarely reading anything. I am way too old for Snapchat so there goes that, and with Tumblr's recent change in adult content policy, you'll never see me there anymore. Follow whatever formula works for you. The only rule is BE INTENTIONAL AND MINDFUL.

So, what's up with a Utility Belt strategy? Here you go, my pretties.

Step 1: Stop believing without questioning everything you see on social media.

Step 2: Sit with the content a minute. How does it feel in your mind and body?

Step 3: Turn off your phone and/or computer for a bit.

Think critically about your social media intake. Look at the content of their other posts. Is there a similar theme? If you see something fishy or something just doesn't feel right, sit with it without internalising whatever message the post may be giving you. Does it feel authentic to you? Lastly, just turn off the damn phone or tablet if all else fails.

CASE STUDY
Chad – The Man Who Had It All Until He Checked His Social Media

Chad was an amazing client and at first I questioned why he needed therapy. On the outside, he had amazing looks, great career, well-proportioned physique, and seemed to have whatever he wanted. But Chad suffered from a massive sense of insecurity and lack. He came from a family of immigrants who instilled this in him, though not on purpose. In processing his family history, he learned they feared losing what they had here in the U.S. as they had lost everything in their native country.

Despite having it all on the outside, Chad never thought he had enough on the inside. A lot of his job involved being active on social media, and he would notice other influencers (God, I hate that term so much; it's so misleading) and measure himself up against their social media strength. He knew on a very superficial level he was excelling, yet every time he checked his stats or someone else's stats, he became disheartened that his presence wasn't as strong as others.

Chad and I had to start dismantling not only his "shoulds" as far as his self-concept but also his measurements of success. He seemed to be the most successful of his family, so not only did he measure his success by others on social media but also by the standards placed on him by his family. We had to rewrite all of the "should" statements he used into "could" statements. Louise Hay, founder of the self-help/metaphysical book publishing company Hay House, once said, "Every time you use the word should, you make yourself wrong." I would add you make others wrong as well. If we change all of our "should" statements to "choose" statements, we eliminate comparison. This took lots of work as our "shoulds" are very well ingrained. Chad would change all "shoulds" to "I choose to," even if he didn't feel it sometimes.

Doing this work on a purely cognitive level began to decrease Chad's overall anxiety and he continued to excel in his career, albeit with much less anxiety. He could look to others on social media for inspiration and ideas, but no longer as a measurement of his success or failure.

Tea Time with Tony

1. *Take a deep dive into what you are using as measuring sticks. See how objective they are. In other words, would someone else whom you know and love use the same sticks?*

2. *Decide to take one day and actually clock the amount of time and times of the day you are on social media. Unless you are a social media person by trade, realistically more than one hour a day is too much.*

3. *As you are practising some of the tricks I outlined above, take a look at your posts. Try to make them as authentic as possible and see how you feel and what kind of response you get.*

4. *Assign which site will be used for what purpose to maintain your sanity.*

Social media is your best friend and/or your worst enemy. You get to choose. You can choose to internalise everything you read and see, leading to you feeling like a piece of shit, or you can change how you consume it. You can also use this as a venue for critical thinking and increased mindfulness. If all else fails, throw your phone and/or tablet out the window.

Have we done enough wrecking? No, as there is so much more wrecking that we can check ourselves on. Time for "Labelling: Check Yourself … Before You Wreck Yourself Even More."

CHAPTER FOUR

Labelling: Check Yourself ... Before You Wreck Yourself Even More

"I don't believe in the Republican party or the Democratic party.

I just believe in parties."

Samantha Jones, "Sex and the City"

Jumping to my spiritual teachings for a moment (yes, I am spiritual AF), one basic thought is that we only have one problem and that's our thoughts of separation. For God's sake, everything has a label or distinction of some sort. I remember when LGBTQIA was just LGBT. Everything has a differentiating label, and we wonder why we are so fucked up?

If we look at advertising campaigns with critical thinking, the subtle ways they increase separation is quite apparent. Advertising is always about the sale. *This product will make you better, stronger, prettier, thinner, etc.* These standards work on folks who see themselves as less than, making them perfect targets for advertisers. Think of an advertising campaign that sells you, "Hey, you are fantastic as you are and there is nothing wrong with you. No one is better than you and you are not better than anyone else. You are just like everyone else in your beauty."

Companies can't sell you something unless they exploit a sense of lack (a side effect of separation). If I feel I lack something, it means that something about me is not enough. Therefore, I really need this product and/or service in order to be enough. We think we are not enough as we are in a constant state of seeing the world from a lens of separation and lack.

> **#OMG Moment:** You don't need anything or anyone to be enough. You are already enough.

Always choose a product and/or service because it appeals to you. Purchase it because you want it to add to your life, not fill a void. So many relationships fail because people gravitate towards them to feel complete. Pay attention to how you feel when you see an ad that catches your eye. Are you thinking, "God, I need that because I will feel better about myself"? Or are you thinking, "This is cool; this would really add to my life (or career, relationship, etc.)"? Pay close attention to that hard sell.

When someone has to work super hard to sell you something and in your gut you are super resistant, listen to that. Present-day coaches and helping professionals who have no business being in the field will use your thoughts of lack and separation to sell you super expensive packages/courses/products that have no data to back up their worth, just their say-so. These are folks who respond to your no by saying, "Well, you need to take a look at that because I am triggering your shadow self and you won't make your goals and dreams happen if you keep saying no to something this good." There is a special place in hell for coaches and helping professionals like these.

> **#OMG Moment:** If something is right for you, a hard sell is not necessary. You will know if it's right for you or not without "the sell".

While there are certainly very competent coaches and helping professionals out there, one can distinguish the good from the bad in what they sell you. The competent ones will just want you to be the best version of yourself possible and recognise that this best version is already there. Essentially, there is no selling. The other kind will sell you something because this is what you definitely need to be the best version of yourself possible. They tell you what that version is. They create students and disciples. They sell you all kinds of shit forever and ever. They essentially suck.

Social media has a big role to play in creating thoughts of separation as well. I will continue to use the term "thoughts of separation" to illustrate the point, not because I believe we are separate. We may be separate as individuals; however, as a species, we are all the same. Social media blatantly breeds separation if we don't use it critically.

I won't go into too much detail about social media as we just talked about this in the previous chapter; however, I just want to remind you that social media is fodder for the biggest amplifier of separation and comparison.

At the core of separation and low self-worth is comparing ourselves to others. When we compare, we become separate by default. There is no way possible that I can compare myself to someone else and not feel separate.

#OMG Moment: When we think we are not enough, or that we are not doing or have done enough, we make ourselves separate from others.

Here's another insidious form of comparison which breeds a massive sense of separation and knocks us out of the present moment: comparing ourselves to a future better version. There is always something we could be doing to improve the quality of our lives. There is nothing wrong with desiring something. To borrow a page from Buddhist philosophy (see how spiritual I am?), it is not our desire for things but our attachment to those desires that causes suffering.

This leads to an examination of the "shoulds" and "musts" in our lives. Famed psychologist Albert Ellis spoke extensively on this matter. In essence, comparing ourselves to a future version is a whole lot of "shoulds" and "musts". I love when clients say to me, "By thirty, I should have had my career on point, a partner, and a house with a French bulldog," or "I must get this job because that is what is expected of me." In what book is that written, folks? We are the authors of our own lives and if we want something, no amount of "shoulding" or "musting" on ourselves will get us there.

> **#OMG Moment:** Shoulds and Musts create lack within yourself. Make choices, not judgements about yourself.

One of the easiest ways of combating our internal "musts" and "shoulds" is by changing the wording we use to describe our internal experience. Would you like to be at another level in your life? Good. Now, what are the steps to get there? *Choose* to take those steps instead of bashing yourself for not being there already. Another Twelve-Step saying, "Be part of the solution and not part of the problem." Staying in your unexamined "shoulds" and "musts" will keep you in the problem and prevent any forward movement from occurring. I teach all my clients that the only thing we ever truly have control over is our choices. We can't always control what we are thinking and/or feeling. We certainly can't control other people.

> **#OMG Moment:** The power of choice is everyone's superpower.

Are you tired of feeling different, separate, not worthy? Make some choices to change that. It can be as easy as changing the wording of your internal dialogue or taking physical steps to feel better. Does this feel overwhelming? Then break it down to meaningful steps. Sometimes goals look and feel like King Size Snickers bars. Our task is to make them into those cute bite-size pieces.

For example, let's talk about fitness goals. Does the thought of going to the gym scare you? Go one day and just sign up. Go for ten minutes the next time you go. Schedule yourself to maybe exercising three times a week for thirty minutes. Goals are only huge in our heads. By breaking them down into smaller steps, even the smallest, you will eventually reach your goal. Confucius said, "A journey of a thousand miles begins with a single step." If we consistently take small steps towards a goal, we will get to the destination at some point. Small steps change the goal from an "if" to a "when".

I mentioned coasting earlier, and now would be a great time to chat about that. When did everything being stable in our lives become such a bad thing? Coasting isn't necessarily good or bad unless we get too familiar with being in a state of coasting, which prevents us from doing the work.

Coasting is necessary for many reasons. It gives us time to settle in to our new way of being. Coasting provides us the time to really integrate new ways of being and doing so it becomes second nature. It can also allow you to be more mindful of the present moment and your internal "enoughness" by allowing you the opportunity to not have to do anything and just be you, all complete and lacking nothing.

> **#OMG Moment:** Outcomes do not determine our worth as a person.

We have become a "results" society instead of a "being" society. Our self-worth is now determined by what we do and what we accomplish instead of WHO WE ARE. The term "rat race" has taken on a whole new level in today's world. We are always chasing after the proverbial cheese. Just like rats, when we are done eating the cheese, the race continues to the next piece of cheese. Just chill out and be you right now.

This all sounds very lofty and unattainable. Not really; it just sounds that way. We may be experiencing difficulties because we grew up with poor role models or even birth-order stuff within our family of origin. (I am the middle child between two girls. It's a wonder I am sane.) From the word go, I had to be the saviour in the family, a place usually reserved for the firstborn. Add on being the child of immigrant parents, and mindfulness was never something taught in my house. Lastly, being a gay boy in the 'eighties was a real kick in the arse with lack of role models.

Even with many accomplishments throughout my life, there was always something driving me to want to do more. While I do look for opportunities to learn and grow, I also take serious stock in being super grateful and happy with who I am today.

When push comes to shove, look to your support system. Grab a trusted friend or friends and ask them what they see in you. Conversely, look at what you see in them. Like attracts like and if you think your friends are bang-up individuals, it means that you are as well. No one likes to hang with Debbie Downer. If your trusted allies believe you are an amazing person, believe them. This is an excellent short-term coping strategy to decrease comparison and increase a sense of wholeness.

#OMG Moment: Surrender outcomes and surrender to who you truly are. Stop punishing yourself by comparing and despairing. That's basic.

Take a good look at yourself and your life. You couldn't have been and done that much bad if you are reading this book. That part of you that longs to be better knows you already are and is nudging you in that direction. We were not put on this Earth for that. We are not being punished by a cruel and unfeeling universe. What sense does that make?

So, when all else fails, here is your Utility Belt Strategy:

Step 1: Ignore the perception of lack.

Step 2: Break the cycle of comparison.

Step 3: Examine your musts and shoulds.

Step 4: Take a deep breath and know you are a fucking rock star.

Don't try to fight the perceptions of lack; just ignore them. Develop the ability to not attach to that voice in your head that tells you you're not as good as so-and-so. This is where the power of choice comes in again. Choose not to follow through with what that voice tells you. If I wasn't able to ignore that self-defeating voice, I wouldn't be where I am right now. Question any "musts" and "shoulds". Change these statements to be less absolute. Search for solutions, not lack of outcomes.

If all else fails, just fucking breathe and know you are a rock star even if you don't feel you are just yet.

CASE STUDY
Chase – The Man With Amazing Friends Who Secretly Hate Him

Chase is such a lovely client to work with, the ideal client, actually. In every session with me, he has no issue being fully vulnerable and hungry for solutions no matter how long it takes to get him there. Chase has had his share of issues, which is why he sought therapy. Because of his past drug addiction, he is in some debt and his job doesn't pay him the salary he needs to get out of it fast enough. He has an amazing support system, in and out of the Twelve-Step meetings. However, Chase constantly questions himself because he feels he is not as good as most folks.

One of his closest friends, Regina, has incorporated Chase into her group of friends. Chase is very happy to be included, yet has this nagging feeling they are only friends with him because of their mutual friendship with Regina. Internally, I am shaking my head as this makes absolutely no sense. I would never be friends with someone I didn't like solely on the recommendation of a mutual friend. Regardless, Chase felt very strongly that this was a possibility.

Upon examining this belief system, Chase felt he had nothing in common with these individuals besides Regina. When I asked him what he did have in common with them, he could only identify the differences and not commonalities. He was so fearful they wouldn't like him that he would not share himself with them as he did with Regina. I suggested to him during his next outing with Regina and company to pay attention to what he has in common with them.

He also spoke very highly of Regina. He trusted her without question and I used this to his advantage. I encouraged him to ask Regina what she thought of him and to sit with the feedback. Clearly, Regina would not bullshit him. This allowed him to believe that she believed, which made the process one of cultivating a sense of connectedness instead of separation.

Tea Time with Tony

1. What do you perceive as lacking in your life and how can you go about changing that without investing an unnecessary ton of money and time?

2. What allows you to sit with information you receive so you can think about it more critically and objectively?

3. What are the "shoulds" and "musts" that dominate your life? Get mindful of what you can do right at this moment instead of beating yourself to a pulp. Sometimes the only thing we can do is change the way we perceive something.

4. What do your trusted allies say about you? If they see the good, what's stopping you from doing the same?

You are unique only in that you are an individual, no better or worse than anyone else despite what they have or what you don't have. Take comparison out of your repertoire of negative coping and start making active choices to have the life you want. Stop "shoulding" and "musting" on yourself. It's not a good look and a surefire way to wreck yourself.

Are we done with the endless cycle of comparison? Have we burned those unrealistic measuring sticks? Good. What an exciting discussion on checking yourself that utilised spiritual, psychological, and pop culture references. Now for something we all need to think about in the next chapter: "From Drama Queen... to Queen Bee."

CHAPTER FIVE

From Drama Queen ... to Queen Bee

"It's not what you think. It's worse."

Dr. Kimberly Shaw, *"Melrose Place"*

Ah, *Melrose Place*. One of my favorite prime-time soaps, second only to *Dynasty* (and I am referring to the original *Melrose Place*, not that horrible remake that lasted one season). After having binged most of the seven seasons of the original this past summer, I was just aghast at how dramatic this show was. Not necessarily the writing, but how the characters responded to shit. It was so over the top and so unnecessary. Basic as all hell. At the same time, so enlightening. We fucking love drama. Yes, you too. You may want to keep a mirror handy as you read this chapter as it's all about you and looking at you.

Ever have one of those mornings where one stupid thing happens and the first words out of your mouth are, "Ugh, this is gonna be the worst day ever," or when something bad happens, you say, "Wow, I am so depressed."? The consistent theme in both these maladaptive statements are the words being used, "worst" and "depressed". In my work with clients, I hear a lot of them say they are depressed. While I honour *what* they are feeling, I challenge them to look at their descriptor words. Are you really going to have the *worst* day ever because you ran out of coffee? Are you really that depressed because they cancelled *Iron Fist* on Netflix? (I minimise the events on purpose).

> **#OMG Moment:** The number-one symptom of the Drama Queen Syndrome (DQS) is the language we use to describe what we are experiencing.

One of the main things I teach my clients and practise myself is to be very mindful of the words we use in describing our feelings and/or circumstances. Words are very powerful, especially in the descriptive sense. Let's take a test. Say something is either "meh" or "awful". Which feels worse? If you are having a bad day and getting all drama queen about it, take a look back at what you have been saying to yourself. What words have you been using? What absolute statements have you been making?

I also find that people throw the word "depression" out like it's nothing. Additionally, they use terms like "I suffer from ..." With established clients, I make them look at this very closely. Are you really depressed or are you just sad? Depression is debilitating in *all* areas of your life, and sadness is part of the human condition. Let's talk about suffering. The definition of suffer states, "to undergo or feel pain or distress". Ask yourself next time you are using that term if you are undergoing or feeling pain or distress. Again, welcome to the chronic illness called the human condition. It is a virus that is with us our whole lives. Alas, suffering is such a great word to get attention and sympathy from others. It's quite dramatic in its application.

Also, in this pharmaceutically obsessed society that we are in, we have fallen passionately in love with diagnosing problems and feeding it a pill. I am continually amazed at the increasing rates of ADHD, a diagnosis that was only recognised in the psychological/psychiatric community in the late 'sixties as "hyperkinetic reaction of childhood". Now, so many adults "suffer" from this disorder as well. Why? Who doesn't want to be on legalised amphetamines all day? Words are getting fancier to become more sophisticated as a society of illnesses. For the vast majority, psychiatric medications create more patients than it does cures. *DISCLAIMER: Before you all try to sue me, never get on or off psychiatric medications without consulting an MD first. Don't go by me. I have a PsyD, not an MD.*

On the topic of diagnosis, the best thing I ever heard was from Marianne Williamson when she said, "All clinical depression means is that someone diagnosed you with depression in a clinic." There is no easy way to say if one meets criteria for a diagnosis or not. Trust me, I have been in the field for half my life. There are too many extraneous variables that come into play. In my work with clients, I let them know from the word go that I don't work with diagnosis; I work with people. I work with clients to help them change their thoughts/feelings/behaviours that are contributing to their needing therapy. If that fits into a diagnosis, it makes no difference to me. I know where my focus needs to be.

> **#OMG Moment:** The only thing to counteract the suffering is to change the way we think about it by changing the words we use to describe it.

Adding to this, way too many people like to use the term, "my depression". Mary, let me tell you something. That is not *your* depression unless you want to be identified by your depression (which, sadly, some people do). Don't own that shit. Say "the depression" instead of "my depression". Do it right now. Using the word "the" makes it much less of a subjective experience, and you are able to do more with something that is outside of you ("the depression") as opposed to something that is this ethereal thing inside of you ("my depression"). Bad news, folks: you can't return "my depression", but you can certainly change how you see "the depression" and make more adaptive choices that aren't quite as dramatic.

Why in the world would we engage in drama and make our lives like a bad episode of *Melrose Place* (most of them were, BTW) on the regular? Why do we like drama? It's very similar to engaging in excessive worrying. Drama gives us a very dysfunctional way to control our experience and potentially problem solve. I am of the belief that what scares us the most is the unknown. Well, when we get all dramatic we may not know the ultimate outcome, but we know what we are doing; we control our present experience by being dramatic, and this leads to the ability to project the fifty-three different disaster outcomes we know for sure will come true. Control and problem solving at its best.

For those of us who don't like to be in the present moment, the dysfunctionality of being a drama queen keeps us firmly planted in the future. Drama mode's focus is purely in the future. It's all about what you think is going to happen.

> **#OMG Moment:** There is no way in hell you can be mindful and be in full-on drama mode.

The most insidious thing about drama is its way of activating our bodies, thereby making us feel something. Have you ever experienced moments in which you wanted to just feel anything other than what you are feeling now? Drama can do that, and it systematically works on so many of our bodily systems in ways that almost make us feel more alive. A good workout and/or shag can do that as well, folks.

Since drama is so normal, being a drama queen normalises whatever experience you are having. We have conversely stigmatised and glorified mental health issues. I think that many people with true mental health issues are scared to disclose due to fear of being labelled a drama queen. Yet, being a drama queen has become commonplace. The dichotomy of this makes my head hurt and my practice full to capacity.

And last, but not least, who doesn't love some attention? I remember an old *Calvin and Hobbes* cartoon strip, maybe three or four panels, in which he is having a temper tantrum and immediately snaps out of it when he sees no one is giving him any attention. Instead of asking for support or sage wisdom from our loved ones, we jump into drama mode because it's easier than asking and it's like getting something for free. Sadly, the cost is really what the drama does to your soul.

Here is your Utility Belt guide to going from Drama Queen to Queen Bee:

Step 1: Do whatever it takes to stay in the present.

Step 2: Remember you ALWAYS have control over your choices.

Step 3: Affirm that negative emotion is normal.

Step 4: Do something physical.

The number-one way to go from Drama Queen to Queen Bee is to stay right the fuck where you are. Our minds will produce a million different worst-case scenarios faster than Donald Trump issues Tweets. These scenarios take us into the far-fetched future like *Star Trek* with little hope of coming back until some damage has been done. Queen Bees know where they are and who they are. Stay present and remember who the fuck you are.

The foundation of everything I teach my clients is that we have control over one thing always and in every situation: our choices. Even in the most horrific of circumstances, you have a choice on how you perceive it. Never will I invalidate when a person is a true victim of a crime; however, at some point, the victim will become their own victimiser if they don't choose to do something to change how they experience this.

Negative human emotions and experiences are completely normal. Being a drama queen is what pathologises this experience. We have grown to actively try to get rid of negative emotions as a whole. Increasing rates of substance use and other forms of addiction are partially the result of an inability to deal with negative emotions effectively because we spend more time covering it up or getting rid of it. We can cover it for as long as we want, but at some point we will have to deal with it. The more we try to get rid of it, the stronger it gets. "That which you resist, persists" is one of my fave sayings. Stop making negative emotions such a bad thing. They are completely normal—whatever normal means, anyway.

And if all else fails, do something physical. This is where we get to have fun. Ever have really angry sex? Aren't those orgasms mind-blowing? I never feel worse emotionally after a good shag or workout. I know yoga is all the latest craze so go do some downward-doggie vinyasa kundalini or something. Anything that requires using your body and/or the five senses will help with getting you back into your body and into the present moment.

A couple of ways that we also benefit from being drama queens involves playing the victim. Drama queen mentality is dysfunctional victim mentality at its core. Why do we play the victim? Because we don't have to take any responsibility while eliciting attention and sympathy from others. It also allows for a psychological protection shield. We can toss people and/or situations aside much easier when we are in drama queen mentality. If it gets too hard, throw that person and/or thing out and move on.

At the end of the day, the real question is: how do you want to show up for your life? What does that feel and look like? If we don't know what that is, how we show up will be chaotic and the world will be chaotic. Do you want to be a drama queen? All right, Mary, but be prepared for consequences.

CASE STUDY
Mark – The Guy Doomed To Be Single For The Rest Of His Life

Mark was the perfect client to walk into my practice. I was in the midst of writing *#IsHeHereYet* and it seemed like I was writing the book for Mark—a middle-aged gay dude who was perpetually single. He always had trouble dating for a significant period of time. We not only had to do a deep dive into what about him was causing his chronic singledom, but also what was he telling himself after every date.

While we did a lot of work on his past issues, one of the things I also like to do is to stay present-focused and look at how he is talking to himself. Not literally, but the language he uses. He would have good first dates. He would have doubts there would be a second date because a reason (insert one of his 103 reasons) would not allow for a second to occur as they wouldn't be interested. He wanted every date to "be the one" and when they weren't, he would get all dramatic with his friends and himself really and ask, "Why me?"

One of the ways Mark and I worked through this was by doing much of the work outlined in *#IsHeHereYet*. However, we had to tackle the Drama Queen Syndrome from a different angle. I challenged him to think of ways he was benefitting from this. Like a good unaware person, he immediately clutched his pearls and denied vehemently that he was benefitting from it. I was only too happy to inform him otherwise.

Getting all dramatic after failed dates allowed him to stay exactly in the very thing he wanted to get out of: being single. Every time he engaged in drama, he eroded his ability to get back on the horse and go back out and try. He also avoided being emotionally vulnerable with another person. Lastly, he got the love and attention he wanted, albeit in a slightly dysfunctional way. His friends would provide solace in his dating drama.

Once he got the Drama Queen Syndrome in remission, he got back on the horse. Last I heard from Mark, he was still single, though actively dating, and his inner drama queen had retired.

Tea Time with Tony

1. *When you are in a bad mood or experiencing some shit, what are the words and phrases you use to describe what is happening and what you are feeling?*

2. *After analysing these words, check to see if there is a way to reword it to make it sound less dramatic or less extreme. Where's there a middle ground for what's going on?*

3. *What are some quick ways to get you present when you are in a heightened state of fear or anxiety?*

4. *Look at the people around you who don't suffer from the Drama Queen Syndrome. See what they do and listen to the content of what they say. This will give you some clues and guidance.*

Are you ready to retire your inner Amanda Woodward and embrace the true, powerful drama-free version of you? Your two biggest weapons in being able to do so are 1) looking very closely at the language you use to describe your experience(s) and 2) staying as grounded in the present moment as possible. While there may be some secondary gain to being the resident drama queen, the result is that you will drive everyone around you bat shit crazy.

Let's look at a subject that is near and dear to my heart and let's get naked. (Well, not actually naked, unless Channing Tatum is reading this book, so please get naked, Channing.) It's time to explore "Stripping Down ... and Getting Comfortable with the Real You" in our next chapter.

CHAPTER SIX
Stripping Down ... and Getting Comfortable with the Real You

"Well, here's my advice. Have a little faith ... and if that doesn't work, a lot of mimosas."

Blair Waldorf, "Gossip Girl"

I feel so compelled to start this chapter with one of my greatest #FML stories (and BTW, all of my #FML moments could fit into one book altogether). There have been two dreams I have had since I can remember: writing a book and going to London. In 2017, I completed and published *#IsHeHereYet*. This led to acquiring the services of a UK-based publicist, the amazing Helen Lewis, who suggested I do a UK publicity tour. As you can imagine, I was in fucking heaven at this point. I'd even get to host a seminar at the London Book Fair about writing for the LGBT audience. Me, one book under my belt, and I'd be hosting a seminar! Like this is a dream come true. Like seriously, only sex with Channing Tatum could top that.

On the day of the seminar, my publicist escorts me to a quick interview prior to my seminar and I serendipitously bump into a senior VP of one of the top five publishing houses. She verbalises interest in speaking with me post-book fair. As my publicist and I leave the room, we both look at each other with such shock and happiness. *Holy crap. Shit just got real.* My publicist transitions into my agent and starts the ball rolling on getting a publishing deal. She has a successful first meeting with the senior VP. My editor and I start to bust our arses on two book proposals and we land a second meeting.

This second meeting with the VP and my agent goes very well and they request a bunch of sample chapters from each book, as well as other information about me. This is all looking very good, right? I mean, publishing contracts never usually start at the VP level. My editor and I bust our arses once again and bang out four chapters (two per book), do a rather extensive market analysis (all my editor's doing), and we are ready to land this book deal. My agent submits the proposal. The senior VP likes it and hands it off to another member of the editorial team. All of us on my side of the street are manifesting and praying and performing African Anteater Rituals (shame on you for not catching the *Can't Buy Me Love* reference). It sounds like a for-sure thing, no?

After about a month of all of us knowing we got this deal, the senior VP came back and said no. The reason wasn't that they didn't like me or my work, but that I didn't have a strong enough online platform to make it as a breakout writer in the competitive world of Self Help. Oh, and my cat became ill with an acute case of pancreatitis the very next day. Major #FML moment.

My emotions at the time left me gutted: lost and now without a sense of direction other than doing what I could to help my cat heal. I couldn't allow myself to fall into deep states of despair as I felt I had failed. I knew where my sadness would take me, and I refused to go there. This series of events was too much of a coincidence not to have been the plan all along. The plan was to get this publishing deal. It all looked fucking good. I thought for sure I was meant to get this deal. Fortunately, I had been cautious about revealing too much, but folks knew something was up. I felt ashamed to tell the few who knew. Ever have one of those dreams where you were in a public place and you were naked? After the news, I felt physically, mentally, emotionally, and spiritually naked, and I didn't know what to do.

The answer was quite simple. So simple, in fact, that all I had to do was do three things: identify the problem, identify the solution, and take the steps to potentially solve the problem with the solutions identified, not knowing if they would work for sure. If I go back and re-read the rejection email, I see they specifically said, "We find his voice intriguing." Therefore, writing style can remain unchanged. They also said, "He doesn't have a strong online presence." Simple solution: increase my fucking followers on social media. (God, I hate that social media is the determining factor in so many things in this world.) My agent and I came up with a plan and I hired a virtual assistant for my actual engagement on social media. While the numbers have been increasing, I am sure it is still not at the level of this publisher's standards at the time of this writing. I have even succumbed to weekly shirtless selfies to get more gay male and heterosexual followers. I will do what it takes short of buying followers.

Here is your Utility Belt Strategy to overcome every #FML moment:

Step 1: Identify the problem.

Step 2: Identify the solution(s).

Step 3: Implement the identified solutions to the identified problem regardless of not knowing what the ultimate outcome is going to look like.

In retrospect, was this a #FML moment? It sure was, as long as I held on to the idea that it was a #FML moment and not another opportunity for me to grow and learn. This experience taught me to stay focused on the "WHY" of why I write. When I wrote my first book, I had little aspirations for a major publishing deal. I just had an idea that I wanted to share with the world. And I did. It lost more money than it made, but the feedback has been worth so much. It also reminded me not to have all my eggs in one basket. Since I was using the Law of Attraction, I knew for sure this was a done deal. I planned my book tour and all that. I got so caught up in the luxury of having this deal that I neglected aspects of my business. This led to a massive decrease in profits and a rude awakening, to say the least. I can go on and on about everything I learned from this #FML moment.

> **#OMG Moment:** The point is really to take any #FML moment and see where you can learn and grow from it, not swim in the self-absorption of negativity that we like to be in.

The reason we think that adversity is a #FML moment is because we see it as a problem. Now, there are certainly real problems in life, like not having food to eat or enough money to pay your bills or some sort of debilitating illness or the death of a loved one. However, even these and other what I call "high-class problems" are all opportunities for change and growth and not always to be thrown in the toilet as a #FML moment.

One of the causes of this is the rapidly developing technology at our fingertips. The use of this technology has allowed for us to essentially not have to work hard for anything. We really don't have to do anything anymore. We can be shut in our apartments for a good week without ever leaving to do anything and have minimal interactions with folks, as everything we need is at the touch of an app. I recently saw an advertisement for an app that delivers liquor. You mean I don't even need to leave the house to get smashed? Yeah! Or not.

We react to the smallest adversities as huge problems because we have become LAZY. There, I said it. We have become a lazy society. I am old enough to know life before Wikipedia, smart phones, and Tinder. When I had a project for school, there was no internet or computer or printer at home to do stuff. I had to go to the Encyclopedia Britannica (what's that? some of you are saying right now) and get the information or pray that the library was still open. There was no texting; we actually talked to people. Dating, well, that was a whole other clusterfuck, but we went out and actually had conversations with people before we engaged in coitus. Technology has basically handed everything to us and we have stopped caring. We want the easier, softer, and immediate solution to everything.

> **#OMG Moment:** All the greatest thinkers and leaders in history have had to overcome their own #FML moments to achieve their greatness.

No one I have any respect for has achieved what they have by having it handed to them. No, they had some major shit and probably the worst #FML moments in human history. Name any great figure in history. Go ahead; I will wait. Now, if you know anything about them, you know that the person(s) you identified had some massive shit go down. Anyone who has ever had anything handed to them without adversity has the respect of the general public for like five minutes (not my five minutes, though). You could go as far as to say that #FML moments build character.

> **#OMG Moment:** I will even say we need so-called #FML moments to grow as individuals.

Let's go back to being naked. No, not right now (unless you're a hot ginger man). I mean when I felt physically, spiritually, mentally, and emotionally naked. Maybe that is exactly how I needed to feel. I needed to be stripped naked on all levels so I could see what needed to get done. By being stripped naked, I got down to the core. My core is that of always doing my best despite the circumstances. I needed the glitz and glamour of this book deal to be taken to get back to basics. There's an old Twelve-Step saying, "If you don't leave the basics, you don't need to go back to the basics." This is what #FML moments can do for you: get you back to the real basic, and not in the way we've been using the word in this book.

Not much growth happens when everything is good, when we are coasting, when it's the start of the fall TV premiere season. The only thing we really do during these times, hopefully, is engage in some mental maintenance. We do the things that keep us in a somewhat balanced state of mind. Or we get so familiar and then comfortable where we are at that we forget what got us good to begin with. #FML moments exist to remind us, not to destroy us. Now give me a major catastrophe, like not getting a for-sure book deal by one of the top five book publishers.

That gives me a psychological boner, let me tell you. Why?

> **#OMG Moment:** #FML moments have all the markings of leveling up, IF YOU CHOOSE TO.

The problem with #FML moments is not the moments themselves but the fact that we don't use them to our advantage. Take this potential book deal. When I wrote my first book, it was a true labour of love. I had no aspirations of a *NYT* bestseller (but I wouldn't have gotten mad if it did become one). I was moved to write the book and share the message. So this chance meeting in London occurs, and all of a sudden, what happens? I forget why I like to write. I have an amazing career as a psychologist in NYC already and have no plans to stop, regardless of my writing endeavors. However, seeing that one of the top five book publishers was interested in me, my mind went to being on stage or on *Ellen* being wooed by Channing Tatum. The years of bullying and low self-esteem would be reversed with this book deal as people would see me as important. I would be lit AF, as the kids would say today.

Losing this book deal—that I never really had to begin with—was a grand #FML moment but also one of my most enlightening moments. When I got stripped naked, I got very present to who I really am and what I want to do.

CASE STUDY
Cameron – The Man With The Dutch Husband, Brazilian Boyfriend, And Lots of #FML Moments

Cameron solicited my services as he was in the midst of a breakup. Now this is almost an everyday occasion in my line of work, but Cameron's initial email did strike me as unique despite it not being comprehensive (I don't fault him for this, as potential clients who give me their entire life story upon first email strike me as needing more than I can give them). In his first session, it was quite evident that he wanted to work, as he was in one of the greatest #FML moments of his life. However, as a psychologist, when a client comes in with a case like this, I get excited.

Cameron had the romance story of a lifetime. Being a single gay man in NYC can pose its complexities. However, when you come to the Big Apple and meet your professional and relationship goals, major win. Cameron met his future husband by random chance after landing the job of his dreams. They took things slowly at first and fell quite in love. Cameron's boo did not have his immigration paperwork to stay very long. After a long discussion and knowing they were in love, they decided to get married. It was a beautiful marriage for about two years and then Cameron's husband's descent into depression and anxiety began. The husband ended up cheating on him and things quickly deteriorated from there.

Cameron leaned on his good friend, a Brazilian man, for support. In a moment of intoxication with alcohol, they ended up in bed together and decided to have this clandestine affair while Cameron started legal divorce proceedings. This did not go over-well with the husband but after many arguments, the divorce was finalised. Amidst all of this, Cameron saw himself falling in love with the Brazilian. As chance would have it, the Brazilian was not very emotionally available for a love relationship and sort of ended it. This led to not one, but two, #FML moments for Cameron.

He was now stripped bare at all levels (and if you saw what the husband did to their apartment, it went up a whole level of nakedness). He literally didn't know if he was coming or going. The best he could do was to show up for sessions and process and cry his arse off. Through the tears and rants, Cameron saw that his greatest weapon to fight this was boundaries. He did not set proper boundaries in his life and the men in his life benefitted from it. Once the boundaries were laid out, Cameron's perspective started to shift from #FML to #OMG.

Tea Time with Tony

1. Make a list of your #FML Moments.

2. Pick one and use your Utility Belt Strategy to shift the #FML to #OMG.

3. Are you able to now see how this was an area of growth for you or your greatest growth experience?

4. What are some of your basics and how can you maintain their use on a daily basis?

After reading all this, I hope that I have at least planted a seed of doubt that we ever truly have #FML moments. We all face these seemingly #FML moments throughout our lives. They are unavoidable. The issue is not that we have them nor how to avoid them, but to use them as a tool for levelling up. These moments are the opportunities where we can really transform and grow, OR stay in a *Telemundo* drama of our own creation.

Follow me to the next chapter, which deals with something probably a tad scarier than #FML moments. Let's have a chat about "Living in the Unknown ... and Finding Your Self-Worth."

CHAPTER SEVEN
Living in the Unknown ... and Finding Your Self-Worth

"Surrender Dorothy".

Wicked Witch of the West,
"The Wizard of Oz"

Picture it: Brooklyn. 2018. It was the best of times; it was the worst of times. There I was, hot off the heels of writing my first book. Things were great. I was feeling really positive about myself and thought, "Hmm, I haven't dated in quite some time." I then embarked on a journey to date again.

I decided to use a less sex-fuelled app this time and matched with a dude about ten years my junior; another new step for me. We immediately connected on all things, comic books as well as cats. We made a date and he got really sick (we FaceTimed and he really was not feeling well). I was going to be travelling over the course of the next two weeks but stayed in touch almost daily. It was super cute. When I got back from my travels, I was like, "Hey, I'm back. Let's have that date." He replied, "So I am not going to be dating for a bit. Between my surgery [which I wasn't aware he was having] and stress at work, I don't have room for dating." Hello, Random Party of One, your table is now available.

A month or so later, on the more sex-fuelled apps, some dude with a headless torso pic (my favourite) hit me up. After I sarcastically asked if he was a model, he sent over a face picture. He was cute, and he seemed genuinely interested in dating. He was also forty years old. We had our first date and, for the life of me, I truly thought he was bored to tears for the first forty-five minutes, but apparently he was just super shy and we hit it off great. We had a second date which went very well too, with two exceptions: he didn't know who Donna Summer was nor did he like the musical Rent. I chuckled, as my former superficial self of long ago would have given him a big ol' "Bye, Felicia". We were both away the following weekend, so we tentatively made plans upon our return. Then, out of the blue, he ghosted me. No explanation. No chance to take him to see *Summer: The Donna Summer Musical*. Nothing.

I sat there wondering, *WTF*? Like, for real. I wrote this great book. I did the work to get to be the best version of myself that I wanted to be, so I should have gotten different results, right? I should have gotten the outcome I wanted, no?

NO. I got the outcome I needed, which was being so okay with me that these two snafus didn't faze me anywhere near as much as they used to. Plus, it gave me greater conviction that no matter what the outcome was and no matter what unknowns I might be facing, the work is always worth it because the work is the outcome.

This brings to mind fad diets. While recognising physiological issues that contribute to obesity, weight loss is more closely correlated to lifestyle changes and not some temporary, trendy diet you saw on Facebook. If you make the choice to eat better (and we all know what that means), we don't have to be on this cycle of diet now, gain weight, oh new fad diet, gain weight, etc. The bottom line is if we maintain the work of eating and being physically active consistently, we don't have to worry about dieting. We are already there.

Clients come to me with miraculous stories of change and progress after putting in the work. Then something happens that brings it all to a sudden halt. They shake their fist at a cruel world and then remember, "Oh hey, I have these tools now." They practise these tools again, then stop *again*, and get the same outcome. This leads to some therapy burnout and possibly dropping out of therapy.

> **#OMG Moment:** The real work isn't the process nor the end result.

The real work is in all of the unknowns when the shit hits the fan *and* when you sashay down the runway of life (or, for my heterosexual dudes, jumping up and down after making the winning touchdown). If we don't internalise this right now, we will be in this never-ending cycle of do the work, get results, stop the work, world comes to an end, and we throw in the towel. The work is in surrendering outcomes, in having faith in ourselves (regardless of religious or spiritual beliefs) that we are worth the work no matter what the outcome is—having faith in ourselves despite the unknowns of change.

I want to share with you the greatest lesson you will ever learn about surrendering outcomes and living in the unknown by retelling a story of someone who did just the opposite. One of the most well-known gay icons is probably Dorothy from *The Wizard of Oz*. She was someone so focused on outcomes that she didn't know her self-worth until the very end of the movie. First, she knows there's a goddamn twister coming and yet she still runs out to find her dog. (I get it. Animal lover and fur dad here.) So she gets sucked into the tornado with her dog and ends up in some strange land having accidentally killed someone. Dorothy is then forcibly given these bling-arse shoes and embarks on a journey to find the Wizard, who she is convinced will have the method to get her back home, along with three companions. Now, the movie could have very well ended had Dorothy gotten the hint in one of the most pivotal scenes from the movie.

Upon Dorothy's arrival in Emerald City, the Wicked Witch of the West flies through the air and, using smoke from her broom, skywrites a very poignant message: "SURRENDER DOROTHY". Did she get the message? Nooo. So, Dorothy continues on this rather dangerous path because she had to have the outcome she wanted. If she had gotten the message, the movie would have ended there, so I recognise the value in Dorothy's continued lack of surrender and self-awareness. At the end of it all, Glinda informs Dorothy that she had the answers all along (at this point, if I had been Dorothy, I would have slapped that bitch for not telling me earlier). This always reminds me that, no matter what we are facing, we have the tools we need within us all the time. Sometimes we just need some crazy witch who probably did too much LSD in the sixties to remind us.

Herein lie so many important lessons. Yes, Dorothy wanted to go home, but her way had to look a certain way and she deviated from the path and endured what she did not have to endure. She ultimately got the result she wanted, albeit putting herself, her friends, and her little dog (too) in danger along the way. When she finally realised she had the wherewithal to go home herself, she came to a better understanding of herself and what she needed to do.

There are some other points I want to make about this classic movie and how it applies to what we are working on here. Yes, like Dorothy, we have to take the tougher path to get to that moment of self-realisation. However, this is always a choice.

> **#OMG Moment:** We can do it the easy way or the hard way. We get to choose that.

The other thing is that the Wicked Witch of the West was really analogous to our voice of fear, as well as those moments of clarity within the unknown. While walking the path we are embarking on, we have that voice that scares us into making poor decisions and/or paralyses us from making those choices. Conversely, in times of clarity, we will also have that subtle message that we need to surrender. These are the times that our true self, the part of us that knows what's up, emerges.

Talk about need for control as a maladaptive way of navigating the unknown. Here's something I've seen (and done) when doing this particular work. We rush, rush, rush to do something because we really want that certain thing. Then, wait … we have to wait sometimes but we hate waiting. We get in this space of funky energy that we don't know what to do with.

So, what do we do? We try to do something else to feel in control over something we don't have control over.

Imagine this (it could have been yesterday for any one of us): we are doing the work and are in this space of unknown results. We feel powerless, nervous, anxious, and/or scared. We don't like any of these feelings; however, we can't always control our feelings. We walk by Magnolia Bakery and think, hmm, a cupcake (or five) will do wonders. We fire up the lovely apps and try to make a connection of some sort with someone. Hey, it's happy hour, let's grab a cocktail (or ten). Oh, Macy's is having a sale. Let's buy all these things that we don't really need. What does all of this binging behaviour boil down to? We hate feeling powerless, we hate the unknown, so we will do everything in our power to control whatever we can regardless of the outcomes. Bam, now we are in control with a lovely hangover or five more pounds or mediocre to bad sex or that lovely Egyptian cotton sheet set we didn't need.

Remember when I said earlier that our minds are like the Wicked Witch of the West? Well, engaging in these binging behaviours to assume a semblance of control on the outside when we feel powerless on the inside is one of the ways the witch speaks to us. It's almost like there is a part of our minds that wants to just fuck ourselves in these rather subtle (or unsubtle) ways. However, let's talk about pouring a bucket of water on this bitch.

For this chapter's Utility Belt method, try this:

Step 1: Slam the brakes.

Step 2: Check yourself.

Step 3: Go back to what you were doing.

Step 4: Surrender outcomes.

Slamming the brakes entails stopping whatever negative chatter and/or control binge behaviour you are engaging in. Before we fall into the avalanche of self-sabotage and despair, STOP. Literally, just stop dead in your tracks. As a general rule of thumb, never make decisions when under a heightened emotional state (unless a car is barrelling straight for you—then, by all means, get the fuck out of the way).

Once you have stopped, engage in the following dialogue: why did I venture into this thing that is having unknown results at the moment? If your motive was wanting to better your life, have the faith in yourself that the work you are doing is always worth it and will lead to some results. It may not look like how you want it to look, but that could be a great thing. If your motives were for some external thing, then you have to re-evaluate why you are doing it and reframe that bad boy quickly. This level of practice requires, at the very least, daily check-ins with yourself. This could take the form of meditation, journalling, yoga, etc. However, the key is in doing something every day that is some form of appropriate self-care.

Now that you have stopped and checked yourself, go back to what you were doing despite having unknown outcomes AT THE *MOMENT*. Remember, the unknown will one day be known (except for maybe why my anti*Rent* date ghosted me).

> **#OMG Moment:** What is known within the unknown IS the process, which IS the work and the result. So STFU and go back to doing what you know IS best for you.

The last step is one of my favourites but also one of the hardest: surrender outcomes. We can certainly want something to look or come out a certain way; however, we need to watch out that we don't *need* it to look or come out a certain way. The want is being in the unknown and not letting it control us. The need is the reverse: letting the unknown control us. (Being in the unknown and not letting it control us.) Don't leave your claw marks on the door frame, folks, but certainly have an idea of what you want.

CASE STUDY
Ray – The Man Who Needed Actions And Immediate Outcomes

Ray came to my office and we immediately clicked. Part of the reason was that he reminded me so much of myself pre-*#IsHeHereYet*. He told me he recently had a breakup in his relationship and was having difficulty in regaining his confidence post-breakup as his ex was already in a relationship and he was "still single".

As Ray and I began our work together, his biggest enemy was his self-dialogue that was plagued with constant comparisons, not only with his ex but his peers as well. Ray would also say things like, "My friend has a much easier time talking to guys than

I do" or "My friends do better on Tinder than I do." The first thing to do was to eliminate this tendency for comparison and own his fierceness. Then I threw him into the fire of going out, socialising, and talking with guys.

At one point, he seemed to master striking up conversations with folks and the like. However, he wouldn't get past the first date. He sat on my couch and complained, "Is it even worth it? I did all this work and I am still single." I reminded Ray the goal wasn't necessarily for him to be in a relationship but for him to regain his self-confidence and be able to be that person he wanted to be. That required constant practice of the skills we had been going over during our sessions. The outcome was never "a boyfriend". The goal and the outcome were the same: being able to show up in the world free of any expectations of outcomes.

Tea Time with Tony

1. *Look at the goals you have attempted but not achieved in the recent past. Now*

challenge yourself to look at what your true motives were.

2. What were those times that you tried something new and you just didn't keep up with it? Why did you stop? No, really, why did you stop?

3. Are you a results-oriented person or a process-oriented person? If you are a results-oriented person, what need are you trying to fill by being focused on how it looks like?

4. What does surrender mean to you?

5. How often do you succumb to your Wicked Witch of the West voice? How can you throw a bucket of water on that?

6. How else can you manage your unease with the unknown other than by engaging in binging behaviours?

These were some tough concepts to look at, no? That is the reason why I threw in *The Wizard of Oz* reference, to make it more tangible and less of a pain in the arse to get through. The work is always worth it. The work is the result. The work is a lifelong daily practice. No pressure, right? Only as much pressure as you *choose* to put on the work. You can continue on the path you want to be on regardless of the outcome because the path is the outcome. The unknown is a space to put on your big-boy pants and bust out fiercely.

Now that we have effectively navigated the unknown and cultivated a greater sense of self-worth, it's the perfect time to chat about transformation in the next chapter, "Transformation ... It's Not Just a Trendy, Spiritual Thing."

CHAPTER EIGHT

Transformation ... It s Not Just a Trendy, Spiritual Thing

"I'm a work in progress! Okay? Maybe I have to get all this b**** out of me before I can be the real me."

Chanel Oberlin, *"Scream Queens"*

"Hi, I am Spiritually Trending Tammy. I am a devotee of that fabulous motivational speaker, Mary Sunshine. I have attended all of these amazing forums and seminars. I do all the forms of yoga in existence and meditate like five hours every day and I have all the answers. I am so convinced I have the answers because Ms. Sunshine said I do because we are all one but some of us shine brighter according to her. I shine supernova bright. I have no problem sharing my truth with you on social media even if you feel shamed by my love and light. I also do all this affiliate marketing so I don't have to work much and sell someone else's hard work and give you mine for free, so I can feel relevant and make money off your insecurities. I am going to align my chakras now because I have worked past my two hours a day that I have set for my spiritual path."

Do you know people like Spiritually Trending Tammy? I do, and fuck them. They give personal development and spirituality/metaphysics a bad name. They go for what is trendy and "the next best thing". The problem with people like Spiritually Trending Tammy is that they usually don't have a mind of their own or their self-esteem is in the toilet and they cling to whatever they find most appealing and what will assuage their sense of low self-worth. It's people like these and other pop-culture spiritualists that give transformation a bad name. But I am here to change that for you. You're welcome.

The good news is, even as you are reading this, you are transforming. Neurochemicals are firing up to send the messages from your eyes to your brain, processing the information you are reading at this moment. You may have visceral responses to some of the themes— more transformation that your body is processing. That kombucha you had for lunch (if you are like Spiritually Trending Tammy) is probably regulating your bowel movements and you may have to poop soon. Poop is food you ate transformed into poop. For God's sakes, people, even poop is a sign of transformation. We are always in a state of transformation.

> **#OMG Moment:** Thanks to social media, affiliate marketing, and other such lovely platforms, we become scared of transformation.

We are scared because we can't achieve the greatness that these folks have achieved or we don't have the money to spend on the programmes/products they are peddling. They make these things sound so appealing, almost too appealing, that it scares me to death.

This leads me to my one of my points: transformation is a personal process. While these seminars and products and books may be helpful guides, what your life looks like cannot be taught by anyone else but you. Even something as simple as a blouse or T-shirt you see on a model or even on a mannequin will not look the same on you because the model and mannequin are not you. You, my beautiful creature, are you. Don't let anyone tell you how it needs to look. It has to feel right.

As I've mentioned before, the problem with these self-proclaimed gurus are that they are not always what they appear to be. They show you, via their advertising and social media, that their lives are so fucking fantastic because of what they do and what they sell. Of course, that's what they are going to show us. Are you going to buy a product or service or programme from someone who says, "Look at me. I'm hopelessly flawed and fucked up. I did this, and it helped a little bit, so please buy it so I can afford therapy services." Of course not. You're going to buy something from someone who's got it going on because you want to have it going on. (Shh ... I've seen some of these gurus beyond the green curtain and let me tell you, they don't always have it going on.)

#OMG Moment: My loves, you already got it going on. You just need to reach in and access it.

The other danger in these products and seminars is they are taught by folks who aren't even certified to do life coaching but because they attended their guru's seminar and their guru said to go forth and coach, all of a sudden, they're coaches. Shit, I wish a guru would tell me I'm Channing Tatum so I can go all *Magic Mike* on the hot boys in Manhattan. So now you're wanting to buy (and often aggressively pushed and/or shamed to buy) this product or seminar from someone who is merely using their life experience, have no education to back up their claim, and have no data or research other than their own word to prove what they are saying is true to take your money and completely improve your life. Sounds stupid, no? Folks, even this book you hold in your hand is just my opinion based on fifty years of living, twenty-six years as a mental health professional, and several decades on and off searching for my personal transformation. I may be full of shit myself, but I am willing to own that.

Please don't send me threatening Tweets about this. I have attended many a seminar and bought products from many competent folks. There are still many gurus whom I love and follow and will continue to do so. Sadly, I have been the victim of being shamed into buying a product or service to change my life for the better. My cautionary rant on the trend of selling coaching programmes and products is just that: use caution.

Take a look back at your life and see all the things you have attempted to do. Did all of them work? Probably not. What did you do when they didn't work? You did things differently or you did something else. Regardless, you probably made it yours.

> **#OMG Moment:** Transformation need never be trendy. It needs to be yours. And it already is.

Conversely, when these things that you tried didn't work out, did you quit? How did that feel? I bet you that you were sitting in harsh judgement of yourself while comparing yourself to others who were engaging in similar endeavours but had different results. So, there you sat in a pool of self-deprecation and loathing, wondering why it couldn't be you. It could have been, but you gave up.

Sure, attend seminars and read books and buy products—with caution. Research these things well.

However, there comes a point when you sound as stupid as Spiritually Trending Tammy, who quotes Mary Sunshine every other sentence because she has no free will of her own. Make these things yours. How it looks in your life will likely be vastly different than how that teacher/author/seller makes it look. The reality is they are no better or worse than you. If they can do it, so can you and their product/service/book will only complement, not create, the transformation you want, as you do have what it takes to do it.

> **#OMG Moment:** I don't believe we live in a chaotic universe. We create chaos pretty well all on our own.

Without getting too much like Spiritually Trending Tammy, I believe there is a certain flow to our lives. If we don't know the meaning of this flow, we can extrapolate the reasons why if we have to ask why. (I personally am not a fan of asking why. Just do it.) That's not to say we sit on our collective arses, eat bonbons, and watch reruns of *The Golden Girls*. We need to do the work to better our lives however we can.

You may be saying right now, "But wait, I didn't ask for this." No, you didn't. (However, Spiritually Trending Tammy would say you used the law of attraction to bring it into your existence.) It's here. You have two choices: take action or practise acceptance.

So, you're scared of taking action? Scared of what the results look like? Scared you don't have what it takes to do it? Let's take a look at all these things. Fear will paralyse us to take action *only* if we let it (unless if you're about to get hit by a truck). Fear of taking action is something we create in our minds. It's not real. It may feel real, but it doesn't actually exist. Most of the things we fear on a day-to-day basis will never happen and, if they should, won't happen nearly to the extent we dread they will or they will happen sometime in the far future. Yes, I can get into all the lovely ways that people have translated the word fear (i.e., False Evidence Appearing Real) but clichés are getting old for me. Fear of transformation and action is not real. We created it and, just as we created it, we can un-create it.

"But I don't know what it's going to look like when I am done." Guess what? You have no guarantees in life. Death and taxes, and that's it. We don't control the results. We only control the choices we make along the way to affect those results. I love working out and I am in full acceptance that I will never look like Channing Tatum and I don't know what the ultimate results will be. However, I love how I feel, and I love noticing the progressive results of my actions. Our envisioned ultimate response may not be what's in our best interest. Ever get something you wanted, exactly how you wanted it, and you ended up hating it? Me too— my last relationship, LOL.

"I don't know how to do this" is the mental trap we fall into that creates sales for these self-proclaimed gurus and life coaches. You may not know the mechanics of how to do something, but you know what you need to do to acquire that knowledge. Researching has become something we can do in just a few keystrokes. We don't even have to leave our beds. Be careful in your research, though, as there are a lot of clowns out there, promoting their own agendas. Seek out several sources as well as asking your friends. Use your voice. Use your fingers. Use your data plan. You will know how to do this.

Now, the hard part. When we take an objective look at transformation and realise there are some logistical things we simply can't change (height, body structure, genetics, etc.), this is when we need to practise acceptance. Acceptance is merely the acknowledgement of what is. I don't have to like something to accept it. I just need to honour that it simply is. Approval, often confused for acceptance, is a personal judgement of like. If I don't accept and I don't approve, then I will surely be miserable. If I accept and don't approve, I can be in a mindset of action towards transformation, as I have now levelled the playing field.

> **#OMG Moment:** Acceptance is not mere passivity calling you to await the thing you want, à la Law of Attraction. It's actively choosing to be okay with something.

I also want to take a moment and talk about the famous Law of Attraction. The problem with LoA (as with most spiritual/religious/psychological dogmas and teachings) is not what it actually teaches, but the followers who fuck it up for the rest of us. At its core, Law of Attraction speaks about mindset, the mindset you need to bring into existence what you want for your life. It's not sitting in meditation for hours at a time and avoiding negative thoughts so you don't attract negativity. It's about consistently transforming your negative thoughts into, at the very least, objective ones to create a new reality for yourself. Be careful when these pop-culture spiritualists throw LoA shade at you. They've got it wrong.

In our quest for transformation, we come across rather serendipitous situations. Here's what I have done in these situations: "IT'S A SIGN FROM GOD." I love when this happens. Yes, it's serendipitous but it's not always a sign from God. Can we simply just take this as something we need to learn from, and not confirmation from our Lord and Saviour? This is another mental trap we engage in to justify our giving up. We see something as a sign from God; hence, it's now co-signed by God to engage in said transformational activity; activity doesn't elicit the results we want, and hey presto, "God sucks." It's not God's fault you are a moron. As Freud said, "Sometimes an apple is just an apple."

Here is your Utility Belt Strategy for transformation:

Step 1: Does it feel right for you?

Step 2: Are you willing to do what it takes to follow this path?

Step 3: Just fucking do it.

CASE STUDY

Spiritually Not-So-Trendy JJ

JJ came to me complaining of having an ogre as a boss. Session after session, I would hear about how awful his boss was. JJ did make mention of some substance use; however, he failed to mention the extent of it. He was also in a relationship he couldn't stand to be in and was tempted to break the monogamy of the relationship. The reality was that JJ felt stuck and didn't think there was a way out of his horrible boss, bad relationship, and chronic substance abuse.

I often share metaphysical principles with clients, sometimes in lingo that is more relatable as this is how it resonates for me. One session, I flat out said, "Spirit, help me see this differently." JJ burst out laughing and I internally clutched my pearls in defence but allowed him to have his moment. We ended the session and off he went.

Things went from bad to worse for JJ. His substance use escalated to the point that he was missing work. His relationship was rapidly deteriorating as a result as well. He ended up losing his job and his boyfriend in a matter of weeks. Defeated, he came into my office and said, "How can Spirit interpret this? Because I just don't know."

My job was now to empower JJ to dig deep and look at the skills he already had as well as to find the appropriate resources. JJ questioned his ability to do any transformation as he had just royally fucked up his life. He felt other people could do it, but he just couldn't. Slowly but surely, JJ took leaps of faith into what he could do to transform, despite being super scared of the outcome. He persisted.

Today JJ has been sober for a few years. While he attends AA meetings, he applies these principles in a way that's real for him. He got this amazing job at a new agency and, yes, he has an amazing boyfriend whom I have met and approved of.

Tea Time with Tony

1. *What are the areas of your life you want to transform?*

2. *What's the negative self-talk going on in your head?*

3. *If the negative thoughts are of comparing yourself to these gurus, how are you like them? The reason you are attracted to them is because you see something of you in them.*

4. *Where can you start taking action right the fuck now?*

5. *How does practising acceptance look to you and how can you start applying this now?*

Hurray! Congrats on your transformation or, at the very least, the decision to actively begin your transformation. Our next chapter, "From #FML to #OMG … Practising Gratitude in Your Life", is something else closely related to transformation that you can use to STFU and show up for yourself.

CHAPTER NINE

From #FML to #OMG ... Practising Gratitude in Your Life

"People waste their time pondering whether a glass is half empty or half full.

Me, I just drink whatever's in the glass."

Sophia Petrillo, "The Golden Girls"

"Want to get high? Write a gratitude list." This is something you will hear frequently in most Twelve-Step fellowships like Alcoholics Anonymous. While it is not a bad philosophy to promote, it does have some flaws. People throw the word gratitude around at the most inopportune moments. However, if you don't use gratitude, you will likely go all Kimberly Shaw on

Melrose Place by throwing off your wig and blowing up an apartment complex full of thirty-year-olds playing twenty-year-olds. In seeking to go from #FML to #OMG, we can benefit greatly from using gratitude as long as we remember one thing: it's a tool.

#OMG Moment: Gratitude is very powerful, but it's not a cure-all.

We just can't slap gratitude over something painful or atrocious because then we are bypassing normal human experience. It's like putting whipped cream over a pile of poop and calling it a sundae. The problem with today's society, which contributes to our inability to go from #FML to #OMG, is that we medicate normal human emotions or want to bypass them altogether because "it's too much". We do this by taking actual medication (don't get me started again because I don't want to be sued). We also do this by overindulging in certain behaviours. However, we also do it by bypassing and minimising it, trying to be all spiritual about it because being pissed the fuck off or feeling super down about something apparently isn't spiritual.

We have forgotten to feel, to feel these feelings and manage said feelings. We go from feeling to solution or medication with no in-between. The pharmaceutical industry is effectively castrating our ability to feel our feelings—and I am referring to normal human emotion, not mental illness. Advertising is all geared towards making you feel better, and covertly making you feel bad by not doing or buying what they are peddling. Shit, even the metaphysical community is churning out some spiritually enlightened bitches who tend to preach how folks shouldn't feel a certain way because that is what you are going to attract and therefore you are wrong for feeling what you are feeling.

> **#OMG Moment:** We have lost our ability to feel, folks. This is why we say #FML so much.

We say #FML because we don't know how to handle negative emotions and we always look to increase the positive emotions. Here is a key tool regarding transformation: negative emotions can be your greatest ally in your transformation process. What? Depression can help us change? Yeah, and you're likely not that depressed, but since sadness is considered to be so negative, we label it depression as this term is more mainstream and garners more attention from others (except me).

Who doesn't love a good drama? As an adolescent, I loved Joan Collins's portrayal of Alexis Morell Carrington Colby Dexter Rowan on *Dynasty*. Everything was so over the top and she was the definition of "extra" these days. I loved every second of her on-screen time. The show was quite the piece of shit prior to her arrival in season two. Our favourite part of any type of media we consume is the drama. Are we ever moved by opening and/or closing credits? No. Are we moved by the day-to-day adventures of our favourite characters? Not really. However, a good lily pond fight or death/resurrection makes all the difference in the world.

#OMG Moment: Drama feels so good in the moment, but makes you so basic.

We don't seem to care if it is good attention or bad attention. Attention is attention and we love it. When we say we are depressed, doesn't that get us more attention than saying we are merely sad? A day does not go by that I don't hear someone say that they are depressed when they are just really sad. Folks, there's a difference.

Without getting too technical, Major Depressive Disorder (otherwise known as depression) can be quite debilitating. On a day-to-day basis, most of us experience sadness, which is a basic human emotion. Sadness is totally tolerable even though it sucks balls while you're going through it. With enough affirmative talk, self-care, and a good friend (or group of friends) to help you navigate it, you will be on the other side in no time. No need for any kind of lost weekend to get you through it.

The main problem is that we do not recognise the normality of human emotions. We all have primary emotions: happiness, sadness, fear, and worry. All mammals feel these emotions. We humans complicated the primary emotions, as we have this wonderful thing called a frontal lobe which allows us to judge and label the fuck out of anything. Our frontal lobe works for us if we take a moment to recognise the feeling we are having and choose differently.

Using any negative thought, feeling, and/or situation as a transformation tool may take some practice and here is where gratitude plays a major role. I don't believe in the randomness of life. Life is only as random as we make it. Therefore, there is some order to how things flow in our lives, including the bad shit. Our reality is not necessarily based on real-life events but our perception of said events. We control perception. Therefore, we can choose to see even the shittiest of situations differently. Using gratitude will help make the shift from #FML to #OMG.

> **#OMG Moment:** What? We get to choose how we perceive even the most horrible shit in our lives? Yes, we do.

My father died when I was twenty-nine years old from a sudden and massive heart attack. So much of my identity was wrapped up in my relationship with my father. Now he was gone from this realm. For the following year, I ate and smoked (cigarettes) through the pain (fortunately, this came during the time I was sober from alcohol or you can imagine what I would have done). I looked in the mirror one day and was absolutely disgusted with how I looked. I was thirty pounds overweight and I swear my complexion was ash from the cigarette smoking. I didn't know who I was without my father. It was one of the most #FML periods of my life.

I looked around my life and was grateful for all the things I had and all the things I had been able to accomplish. And guess what happened? I realised they were not tied to my father. Most of what I was grateful for were things I had done all on my own. Practising what I preached, I decided to make some major changes. I was able to use this newfound motivation to make the changes I needed to make and I was able to feel happy again.

Now, I certainly wasn't grateful my father had died. I miss him every day. I did get very grateful for the things he taught me and that I knew to implement these lessons into reinventing myself (if you knew my family, you would be grateful about this a great deal, LOL). I didn't dishonour my feelings or the year of self-indulgence in pizza and Marlboro Lights. I did what I did, but it was time to do it differently. This all boiled down to: what did I choose to learn from this and how did I choose to live it?

How does all of this lovely stuff we have just been reading about help us get from #FML to #OMG?

Step 1. Whatever you feel, you feel. Give it a name, but a real name. Don't be a drama queen about it. You are not doing yourself any favours by getting all dramatic about it. If you are sad/angry/worried, you're sad/angry/worried. Honour it. When we name something, we give it less power. Don't engage it by adding on to it. How often during the day can we go from zero to 1065 because of all of the additional thoughts we add to a simple and basic primary emotion? The only way to the other side of a feeling is through it, not around it. Feel, baby, feel.

Step 2. While honouring/recognising your pain, choose to see it from an outsider's perspective. How can you see this differently? This goes back to the whole notion of our negative feelings being the keys to transformation. If we can see it differently, we can learn from the situation. If we learn from the situation, we can then apply it to our lives (or not, but that's on you). If we apply it to our lives, bam! Transformation. Another way to do this is to think about what you would tell a loved one if they were going through the same situation. This may be an easier way at first to make your situation less of a #FML and more of an #OMG.

Step 3. Remember that pesky frontal lobe I was talking about earlier? Well, it has the capacity to make choices as well. Therefore, choose the lesson you want to learn. But be realistic when you are doing so. Make it an empowering message, not one that reinforces your inner Negative Nelly. Use gratitude here as well. Don't do like some morons in the spiritual community do and make yourself wrong for what's going on. They love to say stupid shit like, "Oh, don't feel that way because you are just going to attract more of what you are feeling." Fuck that, folks. Feeling and thinking something in the moment is different from dwelling on something for three years on a psychoanalyst's couch. By choosing the lesson you want to learn and subsequently apply, you are honouring yourself and your feelings in the best possible way and allowing good things to manifest.

Step 4. Live the lesson fiercely. You know I will end everything with being fierce. What's sexier and more empowering than being fierce as fuck? Nothing that I can think of. Nothing more needs to be said here, folks.

Now, in a pinch, here is your Utility Belt Strategy to go from #FML to #OMG:

Step 1: Label the feeling.

Step 2: Feel the feeling.

Step 3: Make a choice about what you are going to learn from it.

Step 4: Take a moment and be grateful.

Step 5: Live the lesson.

CASE STUDY

Natalie – The Superwoman with a Vulnerability for Nail Guns

In my younger days as a substance abuse counsellor, I had the amazing experience of working as the lead counsellor for a new residential substance abuse treatment centre for women. I really had the honour to work with so many powerful women from all walks of life, seeking help with their substance use.

One such client was this lovely woman by the name of Natalie. She was the epitome of Superwoman. She took care of all aspects of the household (I believe herself, her husband, and four children). She was active at her children's school, as well as with local sports teams. She was *the* soccer mum. Natalie was also quite handy making repairs around the house. Unfortunately, one fateful day, she accidentally impaled herself with a nail flying out of a nail gun. She suffered some severe gastrointestinal damage and, after surgery, was prescribed painkillers. After some time, the pressure of her decreased functioning and decreased ability to be Superwoman led to an addiction to her pain medications and subsequent admission into the treatment centre.

I was conducting group therapy that day about changing our perspective on things, even the shittiest, and getting to a space of gratitude. I broke it down into three simple steps: you have an actual event, the possibility of a negative perception, and a possibility of a positive perception. Natalie stood up—quite defiantly, which was unlike her—and said, "How in the hell can I see this nail ripping my life apart as positive?" Fortunately, I had a dry erase board and drew a very poor picture of a stomach. I then asked Natalie to name all the titles she had earned: mother, wife, handyperson, and so on. I wrote all the labels inside the stomach as well as a capital A and a capital B on the very top. I drew lines through all the labels she had acquired, much like that nail went through her gastrointestinal organs. I then told her, "Perception A: you get to be the piece of shit you think you are. Perception B: you get grateful this happened and reinvent yourself. No matter which one you pick, the event remains absolutely the same objectively. How you use it changes exponentially." Natalie sat down and realised if she utilised her power in changing the course of her life by using gratitude realistically, she was able to use this experience to create more balance in her life and even out being of service to others as well as to herself.

Tea Time with Tony

1. *So, reality check: are you a drama queen? No, really, are you a drama queen?*

2. *What do you get from constantly affirming #FML instead of #OMG? Come on, you are getting something out of it.*

3. *What are some ways in which you can get yourself situated into the present moment without resorting to some behaviour you may end up regretting later?*

4. *Would you be interested in writing a gratitude list at least once a week?*

5. *Think back to when you made some really good choices in your life. What did it take for you to make—and follow through—with these choices?*

Are you ready to stop fucking your life? A simple tool such as gratitude will cause that change in perception, which then increases your ability to make more adaptive choices for yourself. However, please don't use it to make yourself wrong or to elevate your status to that of a Spiritually Enlightened Bitch. Be realistic. We can honour feelings. We can label feelings. We can feel feelings and still be perfectly spiritual, sane, and a better person.

Now that you have mastered the ability to go from #FML to #OMG, let's dive into our next section where we look at how to create the life we want in our next chapter, "Making Space … and Receiving What You Ask For."

CHAPTER TEN
Making Space ... and Receiving What You Ask For

"The Law of Attraction is all about carefully avoiding achieving things with your actions so you can manifest things with your thoughts."

Ultra Spiritual JP

Without having any family history of aneurysms, I firmly believe I can trigger one if I were placed in a room full of Law of Attractors and Manic Manifestors. I prefer to call them Pop Culture Spiritualists (PCS). The spiritual/personal development community used to be one of peace, solace, and unity. It has now turned into a battleground of what is the next thing they can sell and who are the next batch of people they can manipulate into buying this new bestselling product.

Therefore they manifest stuff for themselves and convince you their product or service will allow you to manifest your wildest dreams. (No offence to Esther Hicks, who is a lovely individual and teaches some amazing philosophies.) Please tell me there's something to manifest a very naked Channing Tatum in my bedroom.

It's the PCSs that want to turn a fast buck in today's online world that misinterpret the basic principles for their own purposes. These are the folks that turn what Ms. Hicks is teaching into something straight out of an *X-Men* movie. It's sad that, since the dawn of man, whenever a new philosophy comes out some idiot comes in and twists it for their own gain. Yes, sorry, folks, you can't just manifest a naked Channing Tatum with your thoughts. I have tried and tried. It's sad to say that as a result of the immediate gratification of the online world, we have become a lazy species.

> **#OMG Moment:** Manifesting isn't JUST thinking specific kinds of thoughts. It also involves BEING, which comes from CONSISTENT action.

I love when I hear people say, "I want to manifest a four-hour work week." Okay, great. What are you going to do with the rest of your time? Watch reruns of *The Golden Girls* and eat bonbons? Why would this be something we would want to manifest? Because we have stopped believing that taking action consistently and being in that action consistently will garner the results we want, but we have to wait. Or maybe there are just factors that are completely out of our grasp to control.

Remember my failed book publishing deal? Well, I was all Law of Attraction with that one and so were so many of my close friends that were in the know. We all claimed it. We all lived in the result of the completed book deal. I was already planning my book tour. I made post-its that said, "Dr. Tony Ortega, (Publishing House name) author". I did everything the PCSs say you need to do when you want to manifest something.

Two things went awry in this process: first, I allowed myself to get too into my head about it. Things were falling by the wayside in my business and personal life, but it was okay because I had this publishing deal. At times, I became a bit of a snob, to be honest. I STOPPED BEING THE PERSON I WANTED TO BE. I say that in caps as when this dawned on me, the pain of the rejection—of something I never had—was lessened significantly. This was so helpful, as I had just self-published a book about being the person you want to be with.

> **#OMG Moment:** Be in the mental frame of having what you want to manifest, but be careful you don't forget where you actually are and who you want to be in the present moment.

It's almost as we have to not ACT as if, but BE as if. Acting implies a sense of inauthenticity of being. Actors play a role, but it's rarely them. Being implies it's who you are and way more authentic. The ultimate question I put to my clients when they are in a conundrum of what to do is, "At any given time, who do you want to be in this situation?" If they can answer this question, they don't really need me for therapy. If I am being the person I want to manifest, the ground becomes super fertile for that manifestation.

Let's take fitness, which is an easy example to illustrate. My goal would be to get to a certain weight and size. The two easy steps are exercise and nutrition and I set that up on a schedule according to my availability. I start to engage in these steps. I start comparing myself to others at the gym or on social media. I start telling myself I will never get there. This thought then decreases the motivation to engage in the steps. I stop engaging in the steps because I have talked myself out of it.

#OMG Moment: *Being* implies consistency, regardless of outcomes or lack thereof.

There is absolutely no magic in just thinking about what I want to manifest. The greatest action we take to manifest into being what we want is in being that person and being that person consistently, regardless of whether it is happening or not.

For me, it would have meant continuing to work on my books instead of planning my book tour. It was in paying attention to the very important things around me instead of allowing them to fall to the wayside. If I had gotten this deal, I would still need to do these things. Since it was a done deal as we had all claimed it, I stopped being. The thought would have been better not that I had this book deal but that I had this book published. This would be the perfect manifestation thought process to BE in to stay consistent in my BEING.

The second thing I did wrong (I use that term as a pure adjective and not to demean myself) was I forgot there are a multitude of variables I have no control of, nor did I have in mind all the possible extraneous variables that could sway what I wanted to manifest in a different direction. Any scientific study does something with percentages or something like that (I may be Spiritual AF but not Scientific AF) to account for extraneous variables. The extraneous variable here: this particular publishing house cared more about the social media following of prospective authors than on the quality of the work itself. Who knew?

One of the benefits of consistently being the person you want to manifest is that it keeps you in the feeling of having the manifestation. So now we have thought, being, and feeling. If we have an idea of what it would feel like, sure, we will be better able to know when it gets here. But what if it doesn't look exactly like how you imagined but still feels the same or quite similar?

> **#OMG Moment:** The clearer you get about how your desired manifestation feels like, the more able you'll be to recognise when it comes in a different form.

Staying in the feeling consistently will assist in your staying in the being consistently, which then keeps you thinking manifestation thoughts. That is your superpower, my dear X-Men.

Let's talk about dating and relationships again, no? Listen, if it's not making money, dating and relationships, or health and fitness, none of you would be reading books like these so we have to talk about them over and over again.

In my first book, I talked about something called the Manventory. The Manventory is a combination of the words "man" and "inventory." Clever, no? This is a comprehensive yet evolving list of qualities you want in your potential mate. (To my heterosexual male and lesbian readers, Womanventory can work as well. Just doesn't sound as cool.) The reason why I made that such an important point of the second half of the book was to get folks into the habit of being.

If I am being the person I want to be with, I will attract a person I want to be with. Again, the downfall for folks with an inability to delay gratification is we are essentially guaranteed a result but no timeline is given as to when it will happen. One of the greatest lessons from writing my own book was exactly what I intended: being so wildly comfortable being single that having a relationship was no longer a desperation. In the back of my mind, I can hear that voice say, "Look, you're still single. Is he here yet?" He may not be here yet, but I am certainly here. Being in this particular space, I know what it feels like to be wildly okay with myself and will bring someone just like that into my sphere of influence. Each "failed" dating experience since the publication of *#IHHY* has served in providing me information on what it is that I really want in a significant other. This has caused many revisions in my Manventory.

#OMG Moment: Your relationship status doesn't matter. What matters is Are You Here Yet?

The more consistent you are as the being of whatever it is that you want to manifest, the more of a reality it becomes. This isn't new though, folks. While used in different words, the fact remains as I have stated. This is how manifesting works with anything.

If you look back at the things you wanted to manifest but didn't, don't despair. Something the PCSs will tell you is not to think about what you don't want. I call bullshit here because hindsight can be a very powerful tool. What we want to manifest can be one of those evolving things in your life. What you thought you wanted to manifest last year may be vastly different from what you want to manifest this year (this is my last relationship in a nutshell). By looking at how we could have done things differently—so we can do differently today—as well as what we thought we wanted versus what we actually want now, manifestation becomes more of a reality and less of a woo-woo thing that folks online talk about.

For God's sakes, folks, regardless of whether you have or haven't manifested what you want, BE HAPPY NOW.

Since I have made particular reference to superpowers in this chapter, here is your Utility Belt Strategy:

Step 1: Think.

Step 2: Be.

Step 3: Feel.

Step 4: Do.

Step 5: Rinse and Repeat.

Yes, think of what it is you want to manifest. Think manifesting thoughts. Think of the outcome you want. Think, think, and do some more thinking. Then start to consistently be in a state of being of the person who has manifested said goal. Stay on point here, folks, as, should you fall off the beaten path, you are still being in the state of manifestation. The more you are being in this state of manifesting, the more you will feel the manifesting, which increases the likelihood that you will manifest. Continue doing the steps you need to take to make this manifestation a reality. Rinse and repeat.

Vincent – The Artist Who Would Give Up Too Quickly

I really enjoy working with creative types as clients. While it does bring a whole level of complexity to my work, I seem to vibe well with them. Vincent is this amazing local artist who came to me because he was just over it. He was an incredibly talented artist but just couldn't do the art he wanted to do full time and had to resort to doing other art that he didn't particularly care for: male nudes.

Usually by the end of every session I have with a client, I have given them some sort of assignment to do for the next session. The assignment is to get the client in the practice of doing something every week toward their goals. I did the same with Vincent. He had a goal to meet every week and we would process the following sessions. What was his response after reporting the completion of the assignment? "Okay, now what?"

Vincent wasn't thinking, he wasn't feeling, and he wasn't being. He was just doing and complained that he was doing and still not achieving the ultimate outcome. It took quite a few sessions to get him to stop just doing for the sake of doing and start doing some of the other things that would generate income I have listed in the Utility Belt Strategy for this chapter.

We processed painting the male nudes for a bit. This task, while not his fave, allowed him to make ends meet. Plus, while he was not creating exactly what he wanted, he was still creating. With these two, he would have a greater opportunity to do what he wanted to do, albeit more part time than he would have liked. After much discussion, we concluded that the reason he really didn't like doing the male nudes was because he felt he was failing as an artist by painting what he didn't really want to paint. Regardless of what he was painting, he's a painter. Plain and simple.

Vincent has not made it big in the art world yet and he hasn't manifested this huge and/or ongoing gig. What he was able to manifest was more peace of mind and continued love of the painting medium despite the subject matter.

Tea Time with Tony

1. *Look back at what you have wanted to manifest and didn't. By adding the Utility Belt Strategy, what can you now consistently be/do/feel/think?*

2. *What are some of the good things you have manifested in your life that took a while to manifest? What did you do then that you could be doing now? Here's a secret: if it worked then, chances are it will work again now.*

3. *How can you get more present to when you are falling off track with your course? Who can you engage to help?*

4. *What are you telling yourself when you are in a space of not manifesting and unknowns? Now, flip this script and change the lingo around into something realistic and empowering.*

Now, I know no one reading this book is a Pop Culture Spiritualist who preys on the desires of others and promises them manifesting everything they ever wished for. You are my people, who know that the Law of Attraction is not some mysterious super woo-woo power. It takes a lot more than just thinking things into reality—it takes being the person who creates this reality. THINK. BE. FEEL. DO.

Another chapter come and gone. Now for some continued looking at yourself with "Meeting Yourself … in Every Person You Meet".

CHAPTER ELEVEN

Meeting Yourself ... in Every Person You Meet

"The spirits aren't trying to hurt us. They're trying to communicate. You've got to face it. You've got to listen to it. You have to face it."

Sam Winchester, *"Supernatural"*

Have you ever had someone tell you, "Oh, the reason why you are mad is because I am triggering your shadow self." These statements trigger my shadow self to donkey punch the fuck out of these so-called lightworkers. My favourite from these folks is, "Oh, you shouldn't feel that as you'll only draw more of it into your existence." Or how about the self-talk when we tell ourselves this pain we are in is wrong and we shouldn't feel this way? This certainly is not a self-esteem booster.

This speaks to me of the whole misguided notion of intolerance of pain. I am old enough to recall the commercial for Alka-Seltzer which had this lovely jingle that went, "Plop, plop, fizz, fizz, oh, what a relief it is." I would not say this product led to society becoming intolerant of negative emotions, but it certainly helped our media define how we want to live. Discomfort, plop, fizz, relief. We are always wanting to seek something outside us to fix the problem in addition to engaging in complete rejection of anything bad or negative. We have also become intolerant of other people having the experience of pain, so we do what we can, often misguided, to fix them.

Many folks in the spiritual/personal development community like to engage in something called "spiritual (or emotional) bypassing". The term was first introduced by John Welwood, a Buddhist teacher and psychotherapist, and it goes like this: "a tendency to use spiritual ideas and practices to sidestep or avoid facing unresolved emotional issues, psychological wounds, and unfinished developmental tasks." For me, this completely minimises the experience you are having and makes me feel wrong.

In addition to bypassing, most of us were taught to believe negative emotions are wrong and bad. We should not feel this way. This is essentially the worst thing you can tell a person. I teach all my clients that applying labels like good and bad to emotions is not appropriate as it implies that emotions have logic, which they don't. If we take on the perspective that feelings are neither good nor bad, they just are, we would be much better people.

Let's tie this together: the problem with calling out shadow self bullshit (SHADE), spiritual bypassing (MORE SHADE), and making negative emotions bad leads to more separation (see Chapter Four) and not being able to recognise similarities in your encounters with other people. These uncomfortable situations give you the information you need to work for your next up level.

> **#OMG Moment:** Recognising your shadow self is part of loving yourself and seeing the connection with others.

When people throw shade at you (or you at yourself) for your shadow self, tell them, "thank you". Your shadow self contains aspects of you that have sustained you for as long as you have been alive, and also has some great qualities to it. I remember a comedian poking fun at how to make the job of a prostitute more palatable for the corporate world: "having sex with more than one person at one time —able to work in a team setting. Negotiating and collecting fees—assertiveness in getting the job done." Our so-called shadow self is not all bad. Folks that tell you that are probably attempting to elevate themselves to another level because they are too scared to look their shadow selves in the face. This causes separation on both sides.

Rejection of our shadow selves does not promote any growth or healing. If there are aspects of our shadow self working against us, rejecting them will only make them more powerful. Many different kinds of books I've consumed have said, "That which you resist, persists." It's the old adage of "don't think of a pink elephant". What are you thinking about right now, folks?

#OMG Moment: Looking straight at our shadow self instead of rejecting it gives us power and direction.

Think of it in medical terms. A doctor needs to look at a tumour/break/lesion, etc., to know to how to treat and heal it. A doctor doesn't ignore or go around it; he goes straight for it. This is why we say thank you for some flippant so-called enlightened person who says our shadow side is triggered. We get to identify and work on improving it.

DISCLAIMER: While others do hold a mirror to us, we can't negate that at some point they are truly and objectively pissing us the fuck off independent of any unacknowledged shadow self. Ignoring our shadow side is synonymous to spiritual/emotional bypassing. People will pooh-pooh our feelings by scaring us into not feeling that way as we will create more of it. Also, they will make reference to how evolved we are and how we shouldn't be feeling this way. We even do this to ourselves.

#OMG Moment: Instead of bypassing (either self or other directed) the negative emotion you are experiencing, why not sit with it and let it work its way through so that you can actually heal?

Because we have become so intolerant of negative emotions, we rush to get rid of them. There's an old trick in behaviour therapy called paradoxical intention. It states, very simply put, you do the thing you are resistant of to get the opposite result. In real life, if you are having a bout of insomnia, tell yourself, "Great, I'll stay up and read some more," and see how quickly you fall asleep, versus telling yourself "OMG, why can't I fall asleep already?"

Sitting with our negative feelings has become counterintuitive in modern society. I heard a lecturer once say, "We have medicalised normal human emotion." At this rate, I believe we have a medication for just about every negative emotion I can think of or, suddenly, this medication that has been out on the market for centuries now works for something else. Sometimes just sitting with a negative emotion quietly, letting it flow through your head without judgement, then doing something to process it will get you more long-term results than a medication you may be told you have to take for the rest of your life.

#OMG Moment: Don't bypass.
Be a badass.

Sitting with your emotions so as to process and heal is a superpower to cultivate. This allows you to become more tolerant of negative internal states as well as not making yourself separate from others.

We use negative emotions either to elevate our situation to a worst-case scenario (this then gives us attention and validation from others because we are special, and we need it) or to confirm to ourselves and others the belief that we truly are a piece of shit (by identifying with the negative emotion and not with our internal power and connection to others).

> **#OMG Moment:** Feelings are like vodka. It has no taste but, if you drink too much of it, you'll be fucked up. Feelings and vodka are good in moderation.

Instead of focusing on how bad things are, or how much better this other person is than you, or how much your life sucks, why not focus on deeper connections? I am not saying ignore the negative. Allow two thought processes to occur at the same time. Your life can suck at the moment, yet you have amazing friends. You feel overwhelmed with your current situation, yet look at all the things you have been able to overcome in the past, just like the people you love have.

Shadow self, bypassing, good/bad equate to labels and distinctions that prevent us from seeing just how similar we are at our core. It never ceases to amaze me how some of my younger and more attractive clients experience (not "suffer", I hate that term, like really) the same shit I do, albeit in different ways because we are different people. My broken pinkie is going to hurt me more than your broken leg. However, we can certainly empathise with each other as we are both just in fucking pain, and help each other out in any way we can.

You guessed it, folks, it's time for your Utility Belt Strategy.

Step 1: Shadow self to integrated warrior.

Step 2: Bypass to badass

Step 3: Hedonistic/nihilistic to balanced yogi

Step 4: Sing "We Are the World"

162

Whenever your shadow self emerges or is identified, don't stay angry and defensive (maybe I am projecting my shit onto you because that is what I feel). Work on your shadow self to transform into an integrated warrior. So many myths have been told about heroes and heroines incorporating lost aspects of themselves to be strong enough to win the battle.

When you or others try to engage in a little bypass, choose to be a badass. Look at whatever you are experiencing right in the eye and listen to it. See what it is revealing to you. It is revealing something that needs to be taken care of and probably soon. Grab that negative stuff by the horns, look at it right in the eyes, listen to it, and bitch slap that shit into the middle of next week.

Don't be a hedonist and chase the positive emotions only or be a nihilist and stay in the negative ones. Be a balance between the two and be an enlightened yogi master. We can experience positive emotions along with negative emotions. If you shoot for at least neutral emotions, that's good too. Positive emotions are not mutually exclusive when in negative emotions and vice versa.

If all else fails, sing "We Are the World" over and over again. If that doesn't get you out of your head and in a space of deeper connectedness to others, I don't know what will. Seeing the events in our lives as absolutes prevents us from seeing how connected we truly are to each other and not so separate at all.

CASE STUDY

Tony Ortega, MS – The Therapist with a Borderline Personality Disorder Client

(Why can't I use myself as one of my own case studies? It's a no-brainer. LOL.) Picture it: Miami, Florida, 1999. Young Tony Ortega just got his master's degree in mental health counselling and was making buttloads of money at a mental health centre. In walks Kera, a very androgynous-looking female with an extensive drug history, possible bipolar disorder and (undiagnosed) borderline personality disorder (BPD). For those of you unfamiliar with this disorder, as a mental health professional, I find BPD to be one of the hardest disorders to treat along with antisocial personality disorder and narcissistic personality disorder.

I was so enthusiastic back then, wanting to heal the world. Kera took a liking to me even before she was officially assigned to me. As any good borderline patient will do, Kera shared with me all the tragedies of her life so I would immediately feel sorry for her and become attached to her. Someone with BPD can be described as follows: "I hate you. Don't leave me." Kera was subtly working her way there and young Tony Ortega was falling for the manipulation.

Kera and I worked well in the beginning. She was very willing to share but when confronted with stuff she didn't want to hear, she fought back. In my inexperience, I took her push back as a personal affront. She was always wanting to see me and always had some crisis she needed my help with.

One day, several months after my father's death, she came into my office and was quite the mess. I don't recall exactly the content of the conversation. All I remember was getting up from my desk, opening the door to my office, and telling Kera, "Get the fuck out of my office." This did not go over well with Kera or my supervisor. I had never yelled (and never have since) at a client like that, ever. I was quite taken aback by the incident.

At the time, I was pursuing how to be Spiritual AF, Round One. I was still very connected with the religion of my upbringing, so it was an uphill battle. However, one author whom I could connect to was

Dr. Wayne Dyer. He had just published a book called *Manifest Your Destiny*. After the "Get the fuck out of my office" debacle, I had read the part where Dr. Dyer said (I'm paraphrasing), "The people who upset you the most are your soul mates. They allow your soul to grow." Like with any good spiritual book, I got super pissed at it and wanted to throw it at my cat. I choose not to and proceeded to think about what Dr. Dyer had said.

If I took away Kera's BPD (not identifying her shadow self), honoured what I was feeling (rather than spiritually bypassing), and recognised the teaching experience this was (feelings are neutral), I can see the human underneath it all and the teacher she became for me.

Having been bullied and abandoned by others for being gay, I know how important having stable relationships were, as I never really had any. It was scary to become vulnerable with someone, as they have the possibility of leaving. I knew how it felt when someone said or did something that felt like they were leaving me and how scary that was. I knew what Kera was feeling at our core, not at the diagnosis stage. When I was able to connect to her on that deep level, I learned what empathy was.

Kera became one of my many soul mates in life. We didn't work together after that one on one, as my supervisor thought it was in Kera's best interest to work with another therapist. She always did attend my groups, though, and I didn't see her as a person attacking me anymore. She was wounded and hurt like I was, and like we all are to some extent.

I don't know what became of Kera as we lost touch after she left the programme. I pray she is sober and happy.

Tea Time with Tony

1. *What is truly so scary about your shadow self? Is this based on something you know or something you feel?*

2. *How do you shut down or bypass your negative feelings? Sit with them for a bit and see what they are trying to tell you.*

3. *What do you typically do when you are having negative feelings and want to run? Now, do the opposite.*

4. *Start to focus on how similar you are to other people. Make it a habit when you want to start throwing shade.*

No matter how much someone pisses you off, you can look within you to make the connection with the other person, all the while honouring your state of pissiness. The two processes are not mutually exclusive. By focusing on cultivating deeper meaning in our daily interactions, things like identifying the shadow self in others, spiritual/emotional bypassing, and intolerance of negative feeling states become less likely. You can meet yourself in every person you meet. However, that work starts with you.

Grab your tissues, folks, as we are coming to the end. Join me on our last chapter – "Showing Up in the World … and Strutting Your Stuff".

CHAPTER TWELVE

Showing Up in the World ... and Strutting Your Stuff

"If you can't love yourself, how in the hell can you love somebody else? Can I get an amen up in here?"

RuPaul

When I finished and internalised what I had written in my first book, I expected things to shift. Guys would be throwing themselves at me. I would be going on dates and writing a satirical anthology about these dates. I also thought I would achieve some level of notoriety. After many months of waiting (along with the conclusion of a massive legal battle with my sister that left my family forever divided), I sat there asking, "Is it here yet?" That moment led to the idea that prompted the book you're holding right now. The question is never, "Is he/she/it here yet?" The appropriate question is, "Are you here yet?"

In 2016, my coach at the time stated his goal for me was "to be wildly okay with being single and who you truly are". I'd like to be funny and say my goal at the time was consistent dick, yet truly what I wanted was to give and receive love, never fully internalising what was needed is to give and receive love for myself first. You would think I'd know that by now. There is a huge difference between knowing and KNOWING.

Simply knowing is the intellectual part of what is being disseminated to you. You can repeat it back. You can remember it robotically like you would the chorus to "Mickey" by Toni Basil. We all *know* a lot of shit.

KNOWING goes beyond the intellect and goes right for your unmentionables; it leaves you breathless and stays in you like herpes. KNOWING is when the intellect becomes so much more on so many levels. I guess you could say it's less about intellectual knowing and more living KNOWING. It has become you and every aspect of you knows this.

> **#OMG Moment:** The only thing that you will ever need to KNOW is there is nothing wrong with you, and nothing outside you will fix what you think is wrong with you.

The main gist of this book is to stop waiting for something or someone to show up to make you feel better or prompt you to follow your goals or make you feel complete. You have everything you need already to do whatever it is to do about any situation. Many of us have been made to believe we don't. Norms imposed on us by our families, religions, peers, or the general population. We can choose today to not buy into those forced scripts any longer and discover who we are and what is right for us.

Exercise has been a major part of my daily life for the past few years and I have been fortunate enough to work with some amazing trainers. My current trainer, Stan, who is this gorgeous slab of Ukrainian beef, has done wonders by me but it's because he is tough as nails. When I worked with previous trainers, I didn't allow them to do walking leg lunges with me. I refused to do them because I knew I couldn't, and folks would make fun of me as I would likely fall on my ass like Farrah Moan on *RuPaul's All-Stars* season four. Stan would have none of that, despite my protests.

He gave me the instructions on what to do, handed me a fifty-pound barbell, and said "Go." Every fibre of my being said I was gonna fuck it up. Guess what? I did. But guess what? Nobody saw it (that I know of, anyway). I put the barbell down and was holding back tears. Years of bullying have left their scar and when a potential for being ridiculed comes up, I still respond from that place. That time I wasn't picked for dodgeball in the ninth grade came up. The other time I walked four players in a row at a softball game I was pitching for came up. All of it came up. The message was, "You can't do this, and everyone will KNOW it."

Stan was very supportive and just asked if I was okay. I let him know I just needed a minute and reminded myself I could do this. I had everything I needed to accomplish what I wanted. Stan couldn't do it for me. He handed me a forty-pound barbell and I said nope, I'm doing the fifty-pound. This time, in full KNOWING, I accomplished a full set of walking leg lunges with only one minor stumble. I tell you this story to illustrate the power of KNOWING, which allows us to show up so much more powerfully in the world regardless of our circumstances.

Since I started the chapter talking about my relationship status, *single*, I want to spend some time talking about the one thing so many people yearn for to feel complete and whole: *relationships*. It's funny how something with such poor endurance statistics is the most sought-after thing in the world besides money and fame. The desperate longing for love is probably one of the things that prevents us from showing up in the world and strutting our stuff.

#OMG Moment: Being single is a superpower.

I said this in my first book and it is worth repeating: being single is a superpower. Typically, when we are single, we spend enormous amounts of time wishing for that true love. Wouldn't it be great if you spent all that time and energy into working on yourself instead of obsessing over something you don't have at the present moment but will have at some point?

Instead of doing all the courses/seminars, seeing all the astrologers, and reading all the books to get that relationship, why not do the things that you have always wanted to do without having to take a partner's consideration into account? Being single means you answer to virtually no one. This could also be the time for you to work on yourself to be the best version of yourself you can be today so that it lays a more fertile foundation to bring in that romantic partner. We always have a tendency to place our focus outward. However, if you practise KNOWING, you will not need to do so. You will KNOW you have the answers already. You just need to access them and sometimes you need the assistance of a professional or a loved one to uncover that.

I don't know when being single became synonymous with the plague. We are more scared of losing a romantic relationship than we are about losing a friendship. For me, it was a feeling I wasn't like everyone else because they were in a relationship. Looking back, it seems pretty stupid because there were people around that were single. Since being in a relationship was so important to me, I only saw the couples. This goes back to the whole notion of projection is perception. What we feel inside (everyone is in a relationship but me) is reflected to our external experience (only seeing coupled folks).

Ever have one of those friends whom you couldn't stand but had to as they were really good friends with some of your good friends? I did. His name was Luke and in the twelve years I have known him, he has been single for about two point five seconds. Luke was preoccupied with being in a relationship. It's all he ever talked about. My eyes would just roll when he showed up as I had to always defend my singlehood.

One night in particular, I was in a car with some friends. As we stopped to pick up Luke, I joked that it would take less than five minutes for Luke to ask me my relationship status. I was even armed this time, as I was reading a new book about being single. My friends thought I was crazy, as I had just graduated with my doctorate and was in private practice so clearly this would be the first thing Luke would bring up. I am sad to say my friends were wrong and at four minutes and thirty-two seconds, Luke asked me, "So, Tony, are you seeing anyone?" My response was, "Nope, and I am very happy being single. I am even reading this new book called [I forget the name but something along the lines of being okay with being single]." Luke had this look of shock on his face and said, "Come on, who would read that?" Luke is now married to a very rich man, has twin children, and lives in Coral Gables, Florida. I'm still single and wildly okay with it.

> **#OMG Moment:** There is more than one type of relationship.

With so much money being spent on getting a relationship, we forget there are other kinds of relationships out there that we could be nurturing in the meantime. I have the best friends in the world and they have done more for me than any cock I have ever *&%$. Why do we place so much more importance on romantic relationships than friendships? Maybe it's revealing our true selves.

In a relationship, we have a greater tendency to hide our true selves by either omitting information about us to our partners and/or playing a role. In our non-romantic relationships, our friends and family call us on our bullshit quicker than quick. In many ways, our non-romantic relationships know us way better than even our romantic partners.

Fear of vulnerability seems to be at the core of it all. Culturally, sociologically, psychologically, politically, etc., being vulnerable is equated to being weak. Here is where we need to define vulnerability. Being vulnerable, as far as this conversation is concerned, is being your true self and not being afraid to show it. If you have to cry, cry. If you like to collect stamps, show it off. If you love to wear plaid, my eyes will roll, but do it, honey. Whether you are being vulnerable or not, mean people exist in the world and they will use authenticity and/or inauthenticity to talk shit about you. So instead of hiding behind some mask for fear of being taken advantage of, let them *try* to take advantage of the real, vulnerable, fucking awesome you. It won't hurt as much.

Holy Bat Shit, folks, it's time for the last Utility Belt Strategy:

Step 1: Just be.

Step 2: Just do.

Step 3: Just KNOW.

We spend way too much time in the how and not enough time in the be. We search and search for how to change things. Sometimes what we have to do is just show up differently. There's an old Twelve-Step saying, "Fake it till you make it." No, I am not contradicting myself. If we are faking the real us that is already there just buried under the rubble of our pasts and modern society, we are not faking—we are revealing. When you want to go from knowing to KNOWING, just repeat it to yourself over and over again, regardless of what it is. Remind yourself of what you KNOW as much as possible.

Case Study
All of Us—Throughout Our Lives

I pulled a fast one on ya. This chapter's case study is all of us throughout our lives. We bought this great self-help book and we know this will be the thing to make us feel better. We spent the weekend in some basement or stadium attending this self-help seminar that everyone is raving about. We go to foreign countries and receive healing from someone who is later accused of sexual abuse. We go to the gym and lose only five pounds so we stop. A naked Channing Tatum has landed on my bed and I am thrilled beyond words. And when it is all said and done, we are still left with the feelings we are trying to get away from because we did the "do" and "be" but didn't KNOW because we didn't get the long-term results we were wanting. So, we are off to the next external thing that will make us happy.

We forget the most important thing in the personal development/self-help world: you do the work because the work is always worth it. The results are in the action and not just in the outcomes. Every time we do the work, we chip away at the barriers that prevent us from accessing our most dynamic selves. Every step we take does this. Every time we stop, no progress is made in chipping away at those walls. Folks, the only guarantee I will ever give you or anyone else is that at some point, if you consistently do the work to get to your goals, you will achieve them. You have to show up for yourself and let the world see that. Ready for some tea?

Tea Time with Tony

1. *What are those external things you have become compulsively reliant on for your internal happiness?*

2. *How has that been working for you?*

3. *How can you flip the script or even rewrite it, so your happiness is generated internally?*

4. *Stay in a state of KNOWING. Just remind yourself, I KNOW. Do what it takes to stay in this KNOWING state.*

Wait a minute. Did I just finish writing a second book? Damn, I always dreamed of writing just the one, but here's another. I hope that beyond the sass and cursing and obsession with Channing Tatum, you get the main message of this chapter and the whole book. You and only you can bring you happiness. You have everything you need to be happy. Don't be a mindless follower of some teacher or movement. Know that you are just as powerful as the next person and stop relying on anything external to make you happy. Choose to be happy now.

My love to you all …

Dr. Tony Ortega

BONUS CHAPTER
Being Betty White, Extra AF

"It's like life is a giant weenie roast and I'm the biggest weenie."

Rose Nylund, *"The Golden Girls"*

It would feel inauthentic if I didn't conclude this book with two things: a quote from *The Golden Girls* and giving you the most extra Utility Belt Strategy for life. For that, I have decided to channel one of the most extra women in the world, someone who has only been basic when she is playing a basic character, a woman who really does not give AF and clearly is doing something right: Betty White. Not only has she been on several hit TV shows, outlived most of her co-stars, and is a world icon, but no one is more extra than Betty White, in my opinion. So, I present to you a Twelve-Step Utility Belt Strategy according to the philosophies of Betty White. Enjoy.

> **Step 1:** "Why do people say, 'Grow some balls'? Balls are weak and sensitive. If you wanna be tough, grow a vagina. Those things can take a pounding."

Life is hard. There is no way around it. Things don't always come easy, not even if you're Betty White. If we look back on our lives, we have all overcome stuff that we thought we couldn't. Yet we did. Don't be a Negative Nellie and be all doom and gloom all the time. Don't set your standards too low to avoid disappointment. Look at your life—past, present, and future—through an objective lens. Things are only as good or as bad as we allow them to be. Don't be a pair of balls that just dangle there and shrink in the face of adversity. Be a powerful vagina, which has more dexterity and ability to take on a good and thorough pounding. Betty White knows this.

> **Step 2:** "Don't try to be young. Just open your mind. Stay interested in stuff. There are so many things I won't get to live long enough to find out about, but

> I'm still curious about them. You know people who are already saying, 'I'm going to be thirty—oh, what am I going to do?' Well, use that decade. Use them all."

Stay in a constant state of wanting to learn more and grow more as a person. I don't recall who said it but I heard this once and it always stuck with me: "Once I think I know all the answers, the questions change." We will never know it all and we were not meant to know it all. This is what evolving entails—being in a state of receiving new information and ways of being. In Steve Jobs's famous commencement speech, he told the graduates, "Stay hungry." What you don't know now, you can know. Don't worry about time or age. Concern yourself with doing it now. Worry keeps you in a state of not doing. Do you think Betty White questioned accepting the role of Rose Nylund on *The Golden Girls*? Probably not.

> **Step 3:** "The bottom line is, I'm blessed with good health. On top of that, I don't

> **go around thinking, 'Oh, I'm ninety, I'd better do this, or better do that.' I'm just Betty. I'm the same Betty that I've always been. Take it or leave it."**

I feel very strongly that what Ms. White is trying to tell us here is to be you. Be you, no matter what. Modern technology has provided us with the means to access so much that it has sent us into this spiral of comparing ourselves to others and seeking more of what we don't have. All the while, we ignore the great shit we can create for ourselves. Stop being so basic by trying to be someone else. Stop thinking about who you want to be or should be. Be in a state of who you are right now and make plans/goals involving where you would like to be later. Be you and don't give AF. Betty White walks around in a state of not giving AF. She's Betty White. She doesn't have to give AF.

> **Step 4:** "A lot of people think this is a goodie two-shoes talking. But we do have a tendency to complain rather than celebrating who we are. I learned at my

> mother's knee it's better to appreciate what's happening ... I think we kind of talk ourselves into the negative sometimes."

If you go back to Step 1, we know that life is going to suck balls sometimes. Every time we have a bad situation, we want to jump into Drama Queen Syndrome (DQS) and blow it up out of proportion (while recognising there are certain really sucky situations that really suck). This is not being the extra you want to be and we know Betty White does not suffer from DQS. Watch the words you use to verbalise your experience. Honour whatever it is you are feeling without getting all dramatic about it. Know that every negative situation is a possibility for growth *if you choose* it to be. Yes, every single one. Betty has lost the majority of her co-stars and she is still out in the public eye. She is not mourning all the time but celebrating that she is still here, all extra and stuff.

Step 5: "You don't look at integrity. You work at it."

Can I talk some more shit here about folks on social media? The overnight coaches and so-called influencers that lack integrity? Yes, those. We need to stop with the doing less to get more. Why not just do to give and receive? This could be a much better way to stay in integrity. For me, this word means I do as I say. My actions are in alignment with what I say. We fall for some of these coaching/social media scams because we think they are in integrity and we are not. What's not being in integrity is not recognising that you have it all, baby, right here and right now. We are not in integrity when we think we need something outside of us to make us whole and complete. Don't ever be ashamed of being who you are and working hard at being who you are. Please don't ever be ashamed of working hard, *period*. You appreciate what you work at for and at. Betty exemplifies this. She's busted her arse in her career and stands in full integrity, even when her character Rose would say stupid shit or when her other character Sue Ann Nivens acted like a slut (from *The Mary Tyler Moore Show*—and shame on you for not knowing the reference).

Step 6: "I just laugh. Have I got them fooled?"

This one is not a complicated one and it is the most profound of our Betty White Utility Belt Strategies because of its simplicity. We forget to do two things in life: breathe and laugh. We take things way too seriously. Lighten things up. I remember sharing an incident on the train with a girlfriend of mine. Some guy mouthed the word "faggot" to me on the train. I simply ignored it but my friend suggested to laugh at the person next time it happens. It certainly takes away the power of a not-so-pleasant situation. I am not saying don't feel bad about something, but at some point, take a deep breath and laugh. Don't emotionally vomit on social media. Laugh at things as much and as often as possible. Keep a good sense of humour as your main tool in your utility belt. Laughing in the face of adversity is extra AF. Grab a martini and stop caring so much. You never see Betty White being sad. She's always laughing and smiling.

Step 7: "All creatures must learn to coexist. That's why the brown bear and the field mouse can share their lives in harmony. Of course, they can't mate, or the mice would explode."

Unless you are independently wealthy and can move to a deserted island or become agoraphobic and never leave your house, you will always have people to contend with. In NYC, where I live, it's inevitable. Yes, we can have virtually anything delivered to our door, but we still have to see the delivery person. Since we are doomed to not be alone in the world, why not just make it a point not only to coexist but to get along? Sure, get rid of the energy vampires in your life, but make it a point to make true connections. Nothing is sexier in the bedroom than a good connection, and not the genital type. Stop the judging and comparing (or at least significantly reduce it, as I judge like all hell). And just be nice to others on social media. No need to be a Twitter/Facebook/Instagram troll. Betty White doesn't have an opinion on this as she doesn't use social media.

Step 8: "My mother always used to say, 'The older you get, the better you get. Unless you're a banana.'"

Can I just tell you how good it's been for my sex life to be an in-shape fifty-year-old in the gay community? I've had more sex in my late forties and early fifties than ever before. We spend so much time dreading and preventing something that's inevitable: aging. We want to age because otherwise we would be dead. Borrow some of the philosophies from Step 2 and stay curious, stay hungry. What is there that you want to know/experience/feel more of? Aging gives us that opportunity. We are able to do more because we have more time. And don't worry about not having enough time. You have right here and right now. Isn't that time enough? Embrace the now. Betty White does. Betty has made it extra AF to age and to age gracefully.

Step 9: "Friendship takes time and energy if it's going to work. You can luck into something great, but it doesn't last if you don't give it proper appreciation."

The rat race to get partnered is one of the biggest quests in human existence. We focus so much of our energies on not being single. We neglect ourselves and we neglect our friends. We need to work equally on all the relationships in our lives, including the one with ourselves. RuPaul, second in extra only to Betty White, always ends an episode of *Drag Race* with "If you don't love yourself, how in the hell you gonna love somebody else?" Yes, I just repeated one of the quotes in the book, but it's worth repeating. Stop focusing on that romantic relationship. Don't worry about getting the romantic relationship while losing track of all the others. Focus on keeping all the relationships by nurturing all the relationships in your life equally. It's abundantly obvious that Betty White loves herself and everyone else. That's extra.

> **Step 10:** "Facebook just sounds like a drag; in my day, seeing pictures of people's vacations was considered punishment."

I wish I didn't need social media as much as I do. Social media consumption consumes so much of my daily life. It's not even the actual use sometimes; it's the planning and timing and preparing content that fucks me up. So, unless your business (and I mean job) is social media, curtail it as much as possible. You don't need to check your feed every two seconds. Pick up the phone and actually call a friend to see how they are doing. Take a walk in the park and actually meet people and not digital images and stories. Engage in the human race instead of the digital world. It will keep your social skills sharp and intellect heightened because social media can make us quite stupid and who wants to be stupid? For God's sake, Betty White isn't even on social media. She doesn't need to be. She's Betty White.

> **Step 11:** "So you may not be as fast on your feet, and the image in your mirror may be a little disappointing, but if you are still functioning and not in pain, gratitude should be the name of the game."

Here is where we stop looking back and saying basic shit like, "Oh, I wish I could have done this or that." Nooo, change that around right now and say, "You know, I have never done that. What do I need to do to do it?" One of my favourite lines from the musical *RENT* goes, "Forget regret or life is yours to miss." If you haven't done it by now, it certainly doesn't mean than you can't do it now. You're still here, so stop your whining. Change it from what you haven't done to what you are going to do now. Right now, you have everything you need to do what you want. We just need to get kicked in the arse to remind ourselves of that fact. Yes, it's a fact. Stop listening to the "nos" and "I can't do its". Appreciate you today and always. Appreciate that at this very moment, you have what it takes to be extra AF. Betty White is in her nineties and putting herself out there as much as she wants to. If Betty White can do it, so can you.

Step 12: "Everybody needs a passion. That's what keeps life interesting. If you live without passion, you can go through life without leaving any footprints."

Do what you love, no matter what. Why in the world would you choose to be and stay miserable? Why would you do things that keep you basic? Because we have been conditioned to just settle. We are not here to just settle. We are here to have the fucking time of our lives. Please do not take this as an excuse to get all hedonistic on me. I am saying that whatever you do, do it with passion. As Dolly Parton says (and she's a whole lot of extra), "Think of who you are and do it on purpose." (Thank you, Mark Dominic, for the quote. Your *Rain Man* memory has finally been put to use.) If anyone is leaving a footprint in this world, it's Betty White.

At the end of the day, Betty White would listen to what you had to say, hand you a drink, and tell you to STFU. Betty White would just kick you in the arse and say, "Get over yourself." All the leading ladies (like Betty White) and men are not basic, they are EXTRA AF. Stop being the supporting character of your own life. STFU and show up for yourself.